Leviticus

Daily Devotions with Jesus

Leviticus

Holiness, Obedience, and Divine Fellowship
Embraced: A Fifty-Day Devotional

GRAHAM JOSEPH HILL

WIPF & STOCK • Eugene, Oregon

LEVITICUS
Holiness, Obedience, and Divine Fellowship Embraced: A Fifty-Day Devotional

Copyright © 2024 Graham Joseph Hill. All rights reserved. Except for brief quotations in critical publications or reviews, no part of this book may be reproduced in any manner without prior written permission from the publisher. Write: Permissions, Wipf and Stock Publishers, 199 W. 8th Ave., Suite 3, Eugene, OR 97401.

Wipf & Stock
An Imprint of Wipf and Stock Publishers
199 W. 8th Ave., Suite 3
Eugene, OR 97401

www.wipfandstock.com

PAPERBACK ISBN: 979-8-3852-2134-9
HARDCOVER ISBN: 979-8-3852-2135-6
EBOOK ISBN: 979-8-3852-2136-3

VERSION NUMBER 070224

For my godmother, Helen Bullock.

Your prayers and love fashioned my life and faith.

You are the good and faithful servant of God we all should aspire to be.

Contents

Introduction | xi

Day 1
Living Offerings | 1

Day 2
Sacred Everyday | 3

Day 3
Communion of Peace | 5

Day 4
Grace for the Unseen | 7

Day 5
Grace in the Shadows | 9

Day 6
Sacred Commitments | 11

Day 7
Restoration's Radical Call | 13

Day 8
The Eternal Flame of Devotion | 15

Day 9
Life as Offering | 17

Day 10
Reflecting the Sacrifice | 19

Day 11
Generosity of Grace | 21

Day 12
Fellowship of Grace | 23

Contents

Day 13
Sacred Distinction | 25

Day 14
Offerings of Peace | 27

Day 15
Ordained to Serve | 29

Day 16
Sacred Approach | 31

Day 17
Holy Reverence | 33

Day 18
Holiness in Everyday Choices | 35

Day 19
Sacred Moments of Grace | 37

Day 20
Compassion beyond Borders | 39

Day 21
Garments of Grace | 41

Day 22
Restoration's Call | 43

Day 23
Sanctified Spaces | 45

Day 24
Grace-Enabled Purification | 47

Day 25
Living Atonement | 49

Day 26
Anchored in the Sacred | 51

Day 27
Holy Reflections | 53

Day 28
Devoted to Holiness | 55

Day 29
Holiness in Action | 57

Contents

Day 30
Integrity of Holiness | 59

Day 31
Living Holiness | 61

Day 32
Distinct for Holiness | 63

Day 33
Holiness in Practice | 65

Day 34
Pure Offerings | 67

Day 35
Sacred Rhythms | 69

Day 36
The Gift of Sabbath | 71

Day 37
Redemptive Celebrations | 73

Day 38
Firstfruits of Faith | 75

Day 39
Harvest of the Spirit | 77

Day 40
Anticipating Faithfulness | 79

Day 41
Atonement in Action | 81

Day 42
Journey of Joy | 83

Day 43
Eternal Light | 85

Day 44
Sacred Words, Just Actions | 87

Day 45
Rhythms of Rest | 89

Day 46
Grace in Jubilee | 91

Day 47
Compassion in Action | 93

Day 48
Covenant Blessings | 95

Day 49
Pathways of Repentance | 97

Day 50
Devoted Integrity | 99

Appendix 1
Daily Devotions with Jesus Devotional Books and Podcast | 101

Appendix 2
Bible Reading Plan | 103

Appendix 3
Other Books and Resources by Graham Joseph Hill | 105

Introduction

IN THE DAILY DEVOTIONS with Jesus series, Rev. Dr. Graham Joseph Hill guides you through the entire Bible, moving from Genesis to Revelation. Daily Devotions with Jesus podcasts and devotional books show you how each book of the Bible can shape your spiritual life and actions in the world. This is a groundbreaking Bible podcast and devotional book series. See how each book of the Bible deepens your faith and inspires you to follow Jesus in life-changing ways!

Leviticus, the third book of the Bible, nestled between Exodus and Numbers, serves as a spiritual cornerstone for believers seeking to deepen their relationship with God. It is often perceived as a challenging read, filled with ancient laws and rituals that seem distant from today's spiritual practices. Yet, within its pages lies a profound message about holiness, obedience, and the nature of God's covenant with God's people. Leviticus calls believers to a life of sanctity and purity, echoing the divine command, "Be holy, for I am holy" (Lev 11:44–45; 1 Pet 1:16).

This book extends beyond mere ritualistic observance; it reflects on the significance of atonement, sacrifice, and worship. The detailed regulations for offerings and festivals underscore the importance of approaching God with reverence and gratitude. Leviticus teaches that worship is not only about external acts but involves the heart's posture towards God.

The themes of Leviticus, including the Day of Atonement and the Holiness Code, enrich our spiritual lives by reminding us of the cost of sin and the grace that covers it. They point towards the

INTRODUCTION

ultimate sacrifice of Jesus Christ, who fulfills the Law and opens a new pathway to divine fellowship. By studying Leviticus, believers gain insights into God's character—divine justice, mercy, and unfailing love—and how they are called to live in response to God's holiness.

Incorporating the lessons of Leviticus into daily devotional practice challenges believers to examine their lives, encourages them to live out their faith with integrity, and deepens their understanding of God's redemptive plan for humanity. Through Leviticus, we learn the value of consecration, the power of God's presence, and the beauty of living a life that honors God the Father, Son, and Holy Spirit.

Rooted in rigorous biblical and theological scholarship, this devotional encourages a fuller understanding of Leviticus and its relevance in today's world. Each day, readers are invited to meditate on a passage, reflecting on its overarching themes and intricate details. This holistic approach illuminates critical messages often overlooked in cursory or superficial readings.

This daily devotional doesn't shy away from biblical and theological depth. It makes no apology for pushing you to examine the theological and biblical meanings of the chapters you read. However, this journey isn't merely intellectual. It beckons the heart and spirit, urging readers to engage in intimate conversations with God, share the timeless message of the gospel, and be invigorated towards Christ-glorifying action. Drawing from the ancient narratives, readers will find inspiration to advocate for peace, champion justice, foster reconciliation, extend mercy, and actively partake in society's transformation.

Deep immersion in Scripture invariably leads to a more profound understanding of God's word and its implications for our lives. This devotional, rich with thought-provoking questions and guided prayers, catalyzes a deeper relationship with God. As you turn each page, may you be drawn closer to God's heart and spurred on to walk in the footsteps of Jesus. This is the fifth book in a series of devotional books designed to guide you through the

Introduction

entire Bible, nourishing your soul, renewing your purpose, and deepening your theology, contemplation, and action.

Here's what is inside this devotional and how best to use it:

1. The devotional covers the entire book of Leviticus over fifty days.
2. Use this book with the Daily Devotions with Jesus podcast—https://grahamjosephhill.com/devotions.
3. Every day as you work your way through this devotional:

    a. *Read* the Bible passage slowly and prayerfully.

    b. *Listen* to the podcast episode for this Bible passage.

    c. *Reflect* on the spiritual devotional.

    d. *Pray* over the Bible passage and devotional and their meanings for your life and the world.

    e. *Act* on your insights.

Reading this Leviticus devotional alone, with family, or with a group will help you understand the Bible more fully and put it into practice. Get ready to change.

All Scripture quotations, unless otherwise indicated, are taken from the World English Bible.

Day 1

Living Offerings

Reading: Leviticus 1

Leviticus 1, at first glance, seems entrenched in ancient rituals distant from our contemporary spiritual journey. Yet, within its verses lies a profound narrative about sacrifice, holiness, and the relentless pursuit of a relationship with the Divine. This chapter introduces burnt offerings, a voluntary worship act signifying the offerer's complete surrender to God. Through meticulous instructions on how offerings should be presented, we uncover layers of meaning relevant to our spiritual lives today.

The essence of Leviticus 1 points to the necessity of approaching God with a heart of total surrender. The burnt offerings, consumed entirely by fire, symbolize the offerer's unreserved dedication to God. This act of giving up something valuable for the sake of divine worship mirrors our call to offer our lives as living sacrifices, holy and pleasing to God. It underscores the principle that true worship involves surrendering our entire being—our actions, will, and desires—to God's service.

This chapter also speaks volumes about the nature of sin, the cost of atonement, and the pathway to reconciliation with God. The meticulous details of the offerings emphasize that sin is not trivial but requires a serious and thoughtful address. It points to the ultimate sacrifice—Jesus Christ—whose atonement on the cross forever bridges the gap between humanity and God. In this light, Leviticus 1 is not just about ancient rites but is at the heart of the gospel itself.

The implications of Leviticus 1 for Christian living are profound and multifaceted. It invites us to pursue lives marked by peace, righteousness, holiness, justice, and reconciliation, mirroring the holistic sacrifice represented in the burnt offerings. The chapter calls us to a lifestyle of humility and service, recognizing that our offerings to God are not merely ritualistic but a reflection of our daily lives. It challenges us to embody compassion, forgiveness, and love for both neighbors and enemies as our lives become a continuous offering to God.

Leviticus 1 compels us to reflect on the nature of our worship. Are we offering God our whole selves, or are we holding back? It reminds us that true worship is not confined to songs and prayers but is lived out in acts of justice, service, and love. In this way, our lives share the grace and love of Jesus, who empowers and enables us to live by a higher calling.

Big Idea: Live as complete offerings to God, embodying sacrifice through daily acts of love, service, and surrender.

Reflection: First, in what areas are we being called to surrender more deeply to God? Second, how can our daily lives reflect the sacrificial worship described in Leviticus 1, serving as a witness to God's love and grace?

Prayer: Gracious God, teach us the true meaning of worship so that we may offer our lives to you as living sacrifices. Help us embrace humility, service, and love, reflecting your grace in all we do. May our lives bear witness to the sacrifice of Jesus, guiding us in our sojourn of faith. Amen.

Day 2

Sacred Everyday

Reading: Leviticus 2

Leviticus 2, focusing on the grain offering, might initially seem to be merely about ancient ceremonial practices. Yet in Leviticus we find spiritual truths applicable to our lives today. This chapter is not just about the physical offering of grain but symbolizes a profound offering of our lives, work, and the fruits of our labor to God.

The grain offering, devoid of animal sacrifice, stands out for its simplicity and accessibility. It represents the everyday work of the people—bread, a staple of life, offered in acknowledgment of God's provision. This offering, mixed with oil and frankincense, teaches us about the purity and sincerity God desires in our worship and offerings. The absence of leaven and honey, which could ferment, symbolizes an offering free from corruption or sweetness that masks the authentic flavor. In essence, Leviticus 2 calls us to offer our best, unadulterated and pure, to God.

For our spiritual lives, Leviticus 2 reminds us that our daily work and the mundane tasks we undertake can be sacred offerings to God. It challenges the dichotomy between the secular and the sacred, inviting us to see all aspects of our lives as integral to our worship. This perspective encourages us to offer our daily labors not merely to seek personal gain but as acts of devotion to God, recognizing God's sovereignty over every aspect of our lives.

Regarding Christian living, Leviticus 2 encourages us to embody values such as humility, service, and love in our everyday actions. It teaches that our smallest acts of kindness and service are significant to God when offered with a pure heart. This chapter invites us to live out our faith in practical ways, seeking justice, acting with compassion, and serving others, not as a means to an end but as a genuine expression of our worship.

Leviticus 2 points us to Jesus, the bread of life, the ultimate grain offering, given for the life of the world. Jesus embodies the perfect offering, his life a fragrant offering to God, marked by obedience, love, and sacrifice. Through Christ, we are empowered and enabled to live out the lessons of Leviticus 2, offering our lives in service, love, and worship.

Big Idea: Transform everyday actions into sacred offerings of worship through purity, sincerity, and service.

Reflection: How can we transform our daily work into offerings pleasing to God? How can we live out the purity and sincerity symbolized by the grain offering?

Prayer: Heavenly Shepherd, teach us to see the sacred in our daily labor and offer our lives, work, and hearts to you with purity and sincerity. Empower us through your Spirit to live out the teachings of Leviticus 2, reflecting the love and sacrifice of Jesus in all that we do. Amen.

Day 3

Communion of Peace

Reading: Leviticus 3

Leviticus 3 introduces the fellowship offering, a unique form of sacrifice that emphasizes peace and communion with God. Unlike the burnt and grain offerings that focus on atonement and worship, the fellowship offering symbolizes the restoration of relationships, celebrating peace and reconciliation between the offerer, the community, and God. It involves sharing a meal, where part of the offering is burnt on the altar, part is given to the priests, and part is eaten by the offerer and their family, thereby nurturing communal harmony and divine fellowship.

This offering speaks deeply to our spiritual lives today, highlighting the essence of our relationship with God and one another. It reminds us that our faith is not just about personal redemption but restoring and building relationships, living in peace, and sharing our lives. The fellowship offering calls us to a life of communion, where we actively seek reconciliation, extend forgiveness, and live in harmony with those around us.

Regarding how Christians should live, Leviticus 3 challenges us to embody the principles of peace, justice, and love in our daily interactions. It urges us to break down walls of hostility and build bridges of understanding and compassion, reflecting God's heart

LEVITICUS

for unity and fellowship. This passage encourages us to engage in acts of service and kindness within our communities and beyond, extending God's love to neighbors and enemies alike. In doing so, we become living testimonies of God's desire for a world where justice, peace, and love prevail.

Leviticus 3 directs our attention towards Jesus, the Prince of Peace, whose life, death, and resurrection embody the ultimate fellowship offering. We are reconciled to God through Christ and invited into a relationship marked by grace, love, and peace. Jesus enables us to live out the themes of Leviticus 3, empowering us to be agents of reconciliation in a fractured world. His example teaches us that our offerings of love and service are not just religious duties but expressions of gratitude for the peace and reconciliation we have received.

Big Idea: Cultivate peace and reconciliation in all relationships, reflecting the unity and love found in Christ.

Reflection: How can we foster peace and reconciliation in our relationships and communities? How can we live out the fellowship offering in our daily lives, extending grace and love to those around us?

Prayer: God of Peace, guide us to live in the spirit of the fellowship offering, seeking peace, practicing justice, and living in loving communion with you and those around us. Empower us by your Spirit to be ambassadors of reconciliation, reflecting the love and grace of Jesus in every aspect of our lives. Amen.

Day 4

Grace for the Unseen

Reading: Leviticus 4

Leviticus 4 discusses the sin offering, a crucial aspect of the ancient Israelites' worship that addressed unintentional sins—those committed in ignorance against God's commandments. This chapter outlines different offerings for various community members, from the high priest to the ordinary person. It emphasizes that sin affects the entire community and its relationship with God, regardless of one's status or intention.

The sin offering teaches us about the seriousness of sin, even when committed unintentionally. It underscores the need for atonement and reconciliation with God, highlighting God's holiness and the impact of our actions on our spiritual and communal life. This concept is vital for our spiritual lives today, reminding us that our unintentional sins—those moments of thoughtlessness, neglect, or ignorance—still require confession and atonement. It invites us into a posture of humility and self-examination, encouraging us to seek God's forgiveness and cleansing regularly.

Leviticus 4 also speaks profoundly to how Christians are called to live. It calls us to a life of humility, recognizing our propensity to sin and the need for God's grace. This chapter encourages us to foster a community where confession, forgiveness, and reconciliation are practiced, acknowledging that our actions affect our relationship with God and those around us. It challenges us to extend grace and forgiveness to others, just as we have received it from God, fostering peace and unity within our communities.

Leviticus 4 leads us to see Jesus, the ultimate sin offering, who took the world's sins upon himself, including those we commit unknowingly. Through his sacrifice, we are offered forgiveness and the opportunity to be reconciled with God. Jesus embodies the fulfillment of the sin offering, providing a way for us to be cleansed from sin and to live in a right relationship with God and others. His grace enables us to respond to the challenges of Leviticus 4, empowering us to lead lives marked by humility, forgiveness, and reconciliation.

Big Idea: Embrace humility and seek reconciliation for unintentional sins, reflecting God's grace through forgiveness.

Reflection: How do we address the unintentional sins in our lives? How can we cultivate a community of forgiveness and reconciliation, reflecting the grace we have received through Christ?

Prayer: Gracious and forgiving God, we thank you for the forgiveness and reconciliation made possible through Jesus Christ. Teach us to live humbly, acknowledging our sins before you and seeking your cleansing. Please help us to build communities of grace where forgiveness and reconciliation flourish. Empower us by your Spirit to live as reflections of your love and grace to those around us. Amen.

Day 5

Grace in the Shadows

Reading: Leviticus 5:1-13

Leviticus 5:1–13 offers profound insights into sin and guilt, extending the conversation from intentional sins to the subtleties of unintentional or unknown sins. This passage outlines various situations where a person might sin without being immediately aware, emphasizing the importance of confession and restitution once the sin is recognized. It teaches that ignorance does not excuse sin, and awareness brings a responsibility to make amends.

This segment of Leviticus underscores a spiritual truth relevant to our lives: the necessity of mindfulness and integrity in our walk with God. It invites us to consider the hidden aspects of our hearts and actions, encouraging a lifestyle of continuous self-examination and repentance. The passage highlights that our relationship with God is deeply personal and requires honesty in our actions, hearts, and minds. It reminds us that spiritual integrity involves acknowledging our faults and failures, even those not immediately evident to us or others.

In practical terms, Leviticus 5:1–13 informs how Christians are to live in a manner that fosters peace, justice, reconciliation, and love. It calls us to a life of humility, recognizing our need for God's grace in dealing with our sins—seen and unseen. This

LEVITICUS

passage encourages us to be proactive in seeking reconciliation, not only with God but also with those around us. It speaks to making amends where possible and demonstrating a commitment to justice and righteousness in our relationships and communities.

This portion of Leviticus guides us to a revelation of Jesus, the embodiment of grace and the ultimate means through which our sins—known and unknown—are forgiven. Jesus's sacrifice on the cross covers all our transgressions and offers us a path to reconciliation with God. Through him, we receive the strength and grace to confront our shortcomings and the courage to seek forgiveness and make restitution. Jesus enables us to develop lives marked by transparency, integrity, and love, mirroring God's heart for people.

Big Idea: Cherish transparency and make amends, living in the grace Jesus provides for sins known and unknown.

Reflection: How can we cultivate a practice of self-examination in our spiritual lives? What steps can we take to make amends for our known and unknown sins?

Prayer: Gracious Creator, guide us in your light to see the hidden corners of our hearts and lead us to live with integrity and honesty before you. Grant us the grace to confess and make restitution for our sins, drawing on the strength and mercy found in Jesus. Help us to live in peace and reconciliation, reflecting your love in all our relationships. Amen.

Day 6

Sacred Commitments

Reading: Leviticus 5:14–19

Leviticus 5:14–19 shifts our focus to the guilt offering, which is designed for situations where a person has committed a violation against the sacred things of God or has inadvertently failed in their commitments. This section reveals God's provision for atonement in cases where one's sin might not be against another person but against God's holy standards, involving restitution plus an additional penalty. It underscores the gravity of our responsibilities before God, mainly how we handle what has been dedicated to divine purposes.

This passage speaks to our spiritual lives by highlighting the importance of integrity in our relationship with God. It reminds us that our actions and commitments carry weight. The guilt offering is a tangible expression of taking responsibility for our actions, making amends, and restoring the relationship with God that our negligence or oversight might have damaged. It's a call to conscientious living, where we are mindful of our duties to God and the sanctity of our promises and obligations.

Regarding Christian living, Leviticus 5:14–19 emphasizes responsibility, restitution, and reconciliation. It encourages us to live with a deep respect for our commitments to God and one another, recognizing that our spiritual life is not just about personal morality but also about how we honor our obligations to God and the community. This passage invites us to approach our mistakes with humility, seeking to make things right through confession, restitution, and seeking forgiveness, thereby maintaining the integrity of our relationship with God and those around us.

This section of Leviticus connects us with Jesus, who embodies the ultimate guilt offering. Through his sacrifice, not only are our sins forgiven, but the way is also made for us to be restored to a right relationship with God. Jesus's life and death demonstrate the seriousness with which God views our transgressions and the depths of God's love in providing a means for reconciliation. Through Christ, we are empowered to foster lives reflecting this understanding, embracing and extending grace to others in our faith journey.

Big Idea: Honor God by fulfilling your commitments with integrity, embracing restitution and reconciliation through Jesus's grace.

Reflection: How do we view our obligations and commitments before God? Are we quick to make restitution and seek reconciliation when we falter?

Prayer: Almighty God, help us live with integrity and respect for the sacred things you have entrusted us. Please give us the courage to admit our faults and the wisdom to make amends as you have taught us. Through the grace of your Son, Jesus, empower us to lead lives that honor our commitments to you and reflect your love and righteousness. Amen.

Day 7

Restoration's Radical Call

Reading: Leviticus 6:1-7

In the heart of Leviticus, nestled within laws and rituals, we find a profound call to integrity and restitution in Leviticus 6:1-7. This passage outlines the requirements for someone who has committed a wrong against another, emphasizing the need for confession, the restoration of what was taken, and additional compensation. Through this lens, the text reveals a divine insistence on justice, wholeness, and the restoration of relationships.

Understanding this passage requires us to see beyond its ancient context to its implications for our spiritual lives today. It speaks to a radical honesty before God and others, acknowledging our wrongs not just in word but in deed through tangible acts of restitution. This approach to confession and restoration mirrors the depth of repentance—a turning away from sin that is both inward and outward.

The call to restitution in Leviticus is not merely about righting wrongs but points us towards a life characterized by peace, justice, integrity, truth telling, and reconciliation. It challenges us to embody love, humility, and service in our interactions, reflecting the heart of God in how we treat others. This is especially relevant in a world where injustice and broken relationships abound. The passage invites us to be agents of healing and reconciliation, actively working to restore wholeness where there is fragmentation.

Leviticus 6:1–7 directs our gaze to Jesus, embodying divine love and grace. In Jesus, we see the ultimate act of restitution—God's response to the brokenness of humanity. Through his life, death, and resurrection, Jesus restores our relationship with God and each other, offering forgiveness and enabling us to live out the principles of peace, justice, and love. In this light, the passage not only instructs us on how to live but also points us to the source of our ability to do so—the grace and love of Christ, which empowers us to be disciples who pursue reconciliation and justice.

Big Idea: Live out radical honesty and restitution as tangible expressions of Christ's love and grace.

Reflection: How does the principle of restitution and restoration challenge or change our understanding of confession and repentance? How can we, empowered by Christ's love and grace, be agents of reconciliation and justice in our communities?

Prayer: Gracious God, who restores and reconciles, please guide us to live out the truths in your word. Please help us to be honest in our confessions, generous in our restitutions, and relentless in our pursuit of justice and peace. May your love and grace empower us to reflect on your heart, bringing healing and wholeness to the brokenness around us. In Jesus's name, we pray. Amen.

Day 8

The Eternal Flame of Devotion

Reading: Leviticus 6:8-13

In Leviticus 6:8-13, we are invited into the perpetual fire of the burnt offering, a fire that must not go out. At its core, this passage is about constancy, dedication, and the continual presence of the Divine amid the people. It speaks to an unending commitment, symbolized by a fire that never dies, representing God's eternal presence and our ongoing devotion.

This eternal flame prompts us to reflect on the constancy of our spiritual lives. In a world that often values the fleeting and temporary, the call to a perpetual spiritual fire challenges us to maintain a steady, unceasing devotion to God. It's a reminder that our relationship with the Divine is not just for moments of need or specific times of worship but is a continual, living connection that sustains us.

Applying the lessons of Leviticus 6:8-13 to our lives today means embodying faith every moment. It's about finding ways to keep our spiritual fervor burning through practices that nourish our souls and actions that reflect God's love and justice. This passage encourages us to be people of peace, embodying love and humility, serving others with a compassion that never wanes, and seeking reconciliation in a world rife with division. Like the perpetual fire, our faith should be a constant source of light and warmth to those around us.

Leviticus 6:8–13 directs our attention towards Jesus, who embodies and fulfills the unceasing devotion to God and humanity. Jesus's life and teachings show us how to live out this constant offering of ourselves, inspiring us with his love and empowering us with his grace to live a life of unwavering faith and service. In him, we find the perfect example of how to keep our spiritual fire alive, burning brightly with love, compassion, and justice.

Big Idea: Nurture an unending devotion to God, reflecting God's constant presence through a life of love, service, and justice.

Reflection: How can we nurture a spiritual fervor that never dims, reflecting God's constant presence in our daily lives? What practices can help us maintain a steady devotion, serving as a perpetual offering to God and the world around us?

Prayer: Eternal God, who commands the fire on the altar never to go out, kindle within us a perpetual flame of love, devotion, and service. Help us to pursue lives that constantly reflect your presence, guided by the example of Jesus. May our hearts remain open to your guidance and grace. We pray in the name of Jesus, who sustains our eternal flame. Amen.

Day 9

Life as Offering

Reading: Leviticus 6:14-23

In Leviticus 6:14-23, we are guided through the meticulous instructions for the grain offering, a ritual that symbolizes devotion and thanksgiving to God. This passage underscores the importance of remembering and honoring God in the everyday through the very sustenance of life—bread. The grain offering, devoid of leaven and mixed with oil, becomes a fragrant reminder of God's provision and the people's response of gratitude.

This ancient practice beckons us to reflect on how we express our thanksgiving and dependence on God daily. It's a call to recognize God's hand in the mundane and the extraordinary, urging us to offer back to God in specific acts of worship and in the totality of our lives. The grain offering teaches us the significance of giving back to God from what we have been given, acknowledging that every gift and breath comes from the Divine.

Drawing from this, Leviticus 6:14-23 informs how Christians are to live in a posture of constant thankfulness and humility, recognizing our reliance on God for our daily bread. This passage challenges us to see our lives as offerings—fragrant, pleasing, and dedicated to God. It speaks to living out our faith through actions of peace, justice, and love, seeing our service to others as an integral part of our worship. Just as the grain offering was a communal act, our lives of service and love are to be lived out in the community, pointing others to the goodness of God.

This passage leads us to Jesus, the bread of life, who embodies the ultimate offering to God. Jesus's life, death, and resurrection perfectly express love and gratitude to God, inviting us into a relationship of deep dependence and thankfulness. In Christ, we find the grace to develop lives continually offered to God, enabled by the Spirit's love to be disciples who embody compassion, service, and forgiveness.

Big Idea: Live daily in gratitude and service, offering every aspect of life as a fragrant dedication to God.

Reflection: How can we incorporate thankfulness and recognition of God's provision into our daily routines? How might our lives reflect a continual offering to God, marked by service, love, and gratitude?

Prayer: Loving and generous God, who provides for all our needs, please instill in us a heart of gratitude and a spirit of thankfulness for your countless blessings. May our lives be a continual offering to you, reflecting your love and grace in every action. Help us to live in humble dependence on you, serving others with the love and compassion you have shown us in Jesus Christ. Amen.

Day 10

Reflecting the Sacrifice

Reading: Leviticus 6:24-30

Leviticus 6:24–30 is about instructions for the sin offering, a crucial aspect of the ancient Israelite worship system designed to atone for and purify from sin. This passage not only outlines the practical steps for making the offering but also emphasizes the sacredness of the act and the necessity of treating God's commands with utmost reverence. The sin offering symbolizes the seriousness of sin, the cost of atonement, and the pathway to reconciliation with God.

This passage speaks volumes about the nature of sin and the incredible lengths God goes to restore us. It reminds us that sin is a personal failing and a breach in our relationship with God that affects our community. The detailed process of the sin offering underlines the seriousness with which we should approach our transgressions and the repentance thereof. It underscores the need for a heart that seeks forgiveness and transformation.

The sin offering points us towards a life characterized by humility, recognizing our need for God's grace, and striving for reconciliation and peace. It calls us to be people who understand the weight of our actions and their impact on others, urging us towards a lifestyle of compassion, forgiveness, and active love for our neighbors and enemies alike. This understanding fosters a community where justice, service, and love are not just ideals but lived realities reflecting the kingdom of God.

This passage points us to Jesus, the ultimate sin offering, who fulfills and transcends the Levitical system. In him, we see the perfect sacrifice that atones for all sin, offering us a path to true reconciliation with God. Jesus embodies the cost of our sins and the depth of God's love for us, providing a model for living and the means by which we can live this way. Through Jesus's sacrifice, we are empowered to nurture lives of service, love, and humility, enabled by his grace to seek peace and justice in our communities.

Big Idea: Pursue humility and seek reconciliation, living as reflections of Christ's ultimate sacrifice for us.

Reflection: How does understanding the cost of sin and the process of atonement impact our approach to repentance and reconciliation in our lives? How can we, through the lens of Jesus's sacrifice, live out our calling to be agents of peace, justice, and love in our communities?

Prayer: Creator God, who provided the ultimate sacrifice in Jesus for our sins, please cultivate a heart of humility and repentance in us. Please help us to grasp the gravity of our sins and the magnificence of your grace. Empower us by your Spirit to foster lives marked by genuine love, service, and the pursuit of peace, reflecting the sacrifice of Jesus in all that we do. Amen.

Day 11

Generosity of Grace

Reading: Leviticus 7:1–10

Leviticus 7:1–10 offers detailed instructions for the guilt offering, a sacrifice that underscores the restoration of community and God's provision for atonement. This passage highlights not just the procedural aspects of the offering but also the underlying principles of restitution, reconciliation, and the sharing of God's gifts. It vividly illustrates how seriously God takes sin, especially when it affects the community and God's gracious provision for reconciliation and restoration.

This text is a powerful reminder of the cost of sin and the grace of forgiveness. It shows us that atonement is not merely a transaction but a transformation that restores relationships. This passage invites us to reflect on our own lives, encouraging us to seek reconciliation where there is estrangement and to offer forgiveness where there is hurt. It challenges us to view our resources not as our own but as gifts from God to be shared in service to Christ and our community.

Leviticus 7:1–10 calls us to a life marked by generosity, service, and a commitment to community. It teaches us that our actions have consequences, not just for our relationship with God but for our relationships with others. This passage encourages us to live in a way that promotes peace, seeks justice, and embodies love and compassion. It reminds us that our faith is a personal adventure and a communal experience where we are called to support, uplift, and care for one another.

This passage points us to Jesus, the ultimate guilt offering, who takes our sins and their consequences upon himself, offering us a path to true reconciliation with God and one another. In Jesus, we see the perfect example of generosity, service, and love. His sacrifice enables us to live out these principles, empowered by his grace and love to be agents of reconciliation and peace.

Big Idea: Live as agents of reconciliation, generously sharing God's grace and fostering community through Jesus's ultimate sacrifice.

Reflection: How are we practicing generosity and service in our community? How can we contribute to reconciliation and peace, reflecting Jesus's sacrifice daily?

Prayer: Heavenly Provider, thank you for your gracious provision for reconciliation and restoration. Help us to lead lives that reflect the sacrifice of Jesus, marked by generosity, service, and a commitment to community. Empower us to be agents of reconciliation, seeking to restore relationships and to share your love and grace with those around us. In Jesus's name, we pray. Amen.

Day 12

Fellowship of Grace

Reading: Leviticus 7:11–21

Leviticus 7:11–21 expands on the fellowship offering, an integral aspect of ancient worship emphasizing community, thanksgiving, and sanctification. This passage delineates the different types of peace offerings and the conditions for their consumption, underscoring the importance of purity, gratitude, and fellowship with God and among the community members. It highlights the sacredness of the offerings and the necessity of approaching God with a heart that is both thankful and obedient.

For our spiritual lives, this text illuminates the profound relationship between thanksgiving, community, and sanctification. It beckons us to live in a state of gratitude. We can recognize that every good gift comes from above. We can share these blessings in fellowship with others. This sharing is not merely physical but extends to our spiritual lives, encouraging us to support one another in our walk with God and fostering a community marked by mutual love, respect, and sanctification.

Leviticus 7:11–21 calls Christians to a lifestyle prioritizing peace, justice, and reconciliation. It teaches us the value of living in harmony with one another, actively seeking to resolve conflicts, and extending forgiveness. This passage challenges us to embody humility, recognize our need for God's grace, and serve others with compassion and love. In doing so, we reflect the heart of God, who desires Christ's people to live in fellowship and unity, sharing the blessings the Spirit has bestowed upon us.

This section of Leviticus leads us to see Jesus, our peace offering, bringing reconciliation between God and humanity and among us. Jesus exemplifies the ultimate act of thanksgiving and fellowship through his life, death, and resurrection, inviting us into a restored relationship with God and one another. Jesus's sacrifice enables us to live out the themes of this passage, empowering us with his love and grace to be disciples who foster peace, justice, and reconciliation in our communities.

Big Idea: Cultivate a community of gratitude, peace, and reconciliation, reflecting Jesus's sacrificial love in our fellowship.

Reflection: How can we cultivate a spirit of thanksgiving daily? How can we contribute to building a community that reflects the peace and fellowship God desires for Christ's people?

Prayer: Glorious and compassionate God, we thank you for the gift of fellowship and the example of your Son, Jesus, who reconciles us to you and one another. Help us to nurture lives of gratitude, sharing your blessings with those around us. Empower us to be peacemakers and agents of reconciliation, reflecting your love and grace in our communities. May our lives be an expression of the peace and fellowship you offer. Amen.

Day 13

Sacred Distinction

Reading: Leviticus 7:22-27

In the heart of Leviticus, nestled within the broader setting of laws and regulations, lies a passage that speaks volumes about the nature of holiness, purity, and our relationship with the Divine. Leviticus 7:22-27 serves as a profound reminder of the boundaries set forth for the people of Israel, specifically prohibiting the consumption of fat and blood. While seemingly straightforward, this command carries layers of meaning that extend far beyond dietary restrictions.

At its core, this passage invites us to consider the sacredness of life and the respect owed to the Creator of all. The prohibition against consuming blood, the essence of life, underscores a fundamental reverence for life's Creator. Similarly, the restriction on fat, often seen as the best part of the sacrifice, teaches us about sacrifice, surrender, and the prioritization of the divine will over our desires.

These ancient guidelines illuminate a path towards a life marked by holiness and distinction. As followers of Christ, we are called to a similar distinction—not through dietary laws but through how we embody love, grace, and compassion in our everyday lives. The call to holiness is a call to reflect the character of

God in our actions, attitudes, and relationships. It beckons us to a life of integrity, where our inner convictions match our outward practices.

This passage points us towards a deeper understanding of peace and reconciliation. Just as the Israelites were instructed to respect the lifeblood of creatures, we are invited to honor the life and dignity of every person we encounter. This respect for life translates into a commitment to love, compassion, integrity, justice, peace, and reconciliation in our broken world. It challenges us to confront systems of injustice and work tirelessly for our neighbors' well-being, reflecting God's heart for justice and mercy.

In the light of the New Testament, these Levitical commands find their ultimate fulfillment in the person of Jesus Christ. Jesus embodies the perfect sacrifice, offering himself once and for all, not just in adherence to the law but in the overflow of divine love. Through his life, death, and resurrection, Jesus demonstrates the depth of God's love and invites us into a relationship characterized by grace and truth. As his followers, we are empowered by the Spirit to live out these principles of holiness, love, and service in our daily lives.

Big Idea: Live a life of distinct holiness by embodying God's love, justice, and reverence for all creation.

Reflection: How does this passage challenge me to live a life of distinction and holiness in today's world? In what ways am I called to embody God's love and justice in my community?

Prayer: Gracious God, who calls us to lives of holiness and service, guide our hearts and minds as we seek to follow you. Help us to embody your love and compassion in all we do, reflecting your light in the darkness. Give us the courage to confront injustice and the strength to love our neighbors as ourselves. May we live in the fullness of your grace, empowered by your Spirit to walk in the way of Jesus. Amen.

Day 14

Offerings of Peace

Reading: Leviticus 7:28-38

Leviticus 7:28-38 offers a profound exploration of the peace offering and its significance, not only in the ancient Israelite context but also in the spiritual lives of contemporary believers. This section intricately details the procedures for presenting the peace offerings to the Lord, emphasizing the communal aspect of worship and sharing God's gifts.

At the heart of this passage is the invitation to participate in a communal expression of gratitude and fellowship with God. The peace offering, unique among the Levitical sacrifices, symbolizes reconciliation and peace with God, reflecting a restored relationship through thanksgiving, vow fulfillment, or free will offerings. It is a tangible expression of the worshiper's desire to live in harmony with the Creator, underscored by the meal sharing between the offerer, the priests, and, symbolically, God.

This ancient practice beckons us to reflect on the depth of our gratitude and the sincerity of our commitment to living in peace with God and one another. It challenges us to consider how we express our thankfulness and actively participate in the community of faith. The peace offering serves as a metaphor for our lives, calling us to be offerings of peace in a world marred by division and conflict.

Christians must live as agents of peace, justice, and reconciliation. In emulating the spirit of the peace offering, we are invited to engage in acts of service, compassion, and humility, seeking to mend our relationship with God and foster unity and understanding among our neighbors. Our lives become a living sacrifice, reflecting the love and grace we have received.

The ultimate peace offering is found in Jesus Christ, who reconciles all things to himself through his sacrifice on the cross. In him, the ideals of the peace offering find their fulfillment, and through his love, presence, spirit, and grace, we are empowered to live as his disciples. Jesus embodies the peace we long for, offering himself for the life of the world and inviting us into a relationship marked by his peace.

Big Idea: Live as embodiments of peace and gratitude, sharing God's love and fostering community through reconciliation and service.

Reflection: How does my life reflect the gratitude and peace that the peace offering symbolizes? In what ways am I contributing to the communal expression of faith and worship in my context?

Prayer: Eternal God, who has called us to live in peace and gratitude, please empower us by your Spirit to be ambassadors of reconciliation. May our lives reflect the sacrifice of Jesus, the ultimate peace offering, as we seek to build bridges of understanding and love in our communities. Help us cherish the gift of fellowship with you and each other, sharing generously the blessings you have bestowed upon us. Guide us in paths of righteousness, that our lives may be a pleasing offering to you. Amen.

Day 15

Ordained to Serve

Reading: Leviticus 8

Leviticus 8 unfolds the detailed process of ordaining Aaron and his sons into the priesthood, a momentous occasion that signified more than just a ceremonial ritual. It was a profound declaration of God's desire to dwell among God's people and to guide them in pursuing lives that reflect divine holiness and righteousness. This chapter, rich in symbolism and purpose, marks a pivotal moment in the spiritual odyssey of the Israelites, setting Aaron and his sons apart through elaborate rituals that underscore the gravity and sanctity of their appointed roles.

The ordination of the priests, involving sacrifices, anointing oil, and the laying on of hands, symbolizes the profound responsibility of mediating between God and people. It speaks to the seriousness with which God regards the act of intercession and the necessity of purity, dedication, and holiness in those who serve God. This passage invites us to reflect on the nature of authentic spiritual leadership—a leadership rooted not in power and authority but in service, sacrifice, and a deep commitment to living out God's commands.

Leviticus 8 beckons us to consider our calling and ordination as believers. In the New Testament context, this calling is not confined to a select few but extends to all who follow Christ. As Peter describes, we are a "royal priesthood" called to offer spiritual sacrifices acceptable to God through Jesus Christ. This identity invites us to nurture lives marked by the same dedication, purity, and service demonstrated in Leviticus 8, showing God's grace and love in a world desperately needing both.

The themes of peace, justice, reconciliation, love, humility, service, faith, compassion, and forgiveness that emerge from Leviticus 8 inform how Christians are to live in response to our ordination as God's priests. We are called to be agents of reconciliation, working tirelessly to mend the brokenness in our world. Our service is to be characterized by love and humility, seeking not our glory but the flourishing of those around us. In doing so, we embody the compassion and forgiveness that define God's character, extending grace to friends and enemies alike.

This passage points us to Jesus, the high priest, who perfectly fulfilled the roles and rituals outlined in Leviticus. Through his life, death, and resurrection, Jesus embodies the ultimate act of intercession, reconciling humanity to God once and for all. His example inspires us to live out our priestly calling, empowered by his love, presence, spirit, and grace.

Big Idea: Accept your calling as part of God's royal priesthood, living out service, reconciliation, and love in reflection of Jesus's ultimate sacrifice.

Reflection: How does my life reflect the dedication and service required of those the Spirit calls to be God's priests? In what ways am I living out the reconciling work of Jesus in my community?

Prayer: Covenant God, who has called us into a royal priesthood, equip us to serve you with purity, dedication, and love. Help us embody your high priest's virtues, our Lord Jesus Christ, in every aspect of our lives. May our service reflect your heart for reconciliation, justice, and peace. Empower us by your Spirit to be faithful mediators of your grace and love in a broken world. Amen.

Day 16

Sacred Approach

Reading: Leviticus 9

Leviticus 9 captures a moment of profound significance: the first sacrifices made by Aaron and his sons after their ordination, culminating in the glorious manifestation of God's presence among the people. This chapter is not merely a historical account but a rich in symbolism, foreshadowing, and spiritual instruction. It illustrates the meticulous care with which God instructs people to approach God, emphasizing the gravity of sin, the necessity of atonement, and the beauty of divine fellowship.

The central theme of Leviticus 9 is the inauguration of the priesthood and the altar, marking the commencement of the Levitical service. Aaron's obedience to God's precise instructions and the subsequent appearance of God's glory to all the people underscore a truth: God's holiness and our approach to the Divine cannot be taken lightly. This chapter invites us into a deeper understanding of God's absolute purity and the serious nature of our sin, which necessitates a mediator and savior.

Leviticus 9 is a powerful reminder of the cost of sin and the grace of atonement. It compels us to reflect on our approach to God, recognizing the need for sincere repentance and the beauty of God's provision for reconciliation with our Creator. The sacrifices, while specific to the Levitical priesthood, point forward to the ultimate sacrifice of Jesus Christ, our high priest, who offers not the blood of bulls and goats but his blood for our atonement.

Thus, Leviticus 9 informs how Christians should live in several profound ways. Firstly, it calls us to approach God with reverence and awe, mindful of divine holiness and our need for cleansing. It also invites us to embrace the peace, justice, and reconciliation made possible through Christ's sacrifice, encouraging us to extend forgiveness, love, and compassion to others. As recipients of God's grace, the Spirit empowers us to live as agents of reconciliation, embodying Christ's love in our relationships and communities.

This chapter points us unmistakably to Jesus, the perfect mediator between God and humanity. His sacrifice on the cross and his role as our high priest enables us to come boldly before the throne of grace, not based on our righteousness but on his mercy and love. In Jesus, we find the fulfillment of every sacrifice, the answer to our deepest need for atonement, and the source of our hope for eternal fellowship with God.

Big Idea: Approach God with reverence, embracing the reconciliation offered through Christ to live as peacemakers.

Reflection: How does my life reflect a proper understanding of God's holiness and the grace our Creator offers through Jesus Christ? In what ways am I living as an agent of reconciliation, reflecting the peace and justice of God's kingdom in my daily interactions?

Prayer: Gracious and loving God, we stand in awe of your holiness and grace. Teach us to approach you with the reverence and gratitude your holiness demands. Thank you for the gift of your Son, Jesus, who bridges the gap between our sinfulness and your purity. Empower us by your Spirit to live as reconcilers in this world, spreading your love, justice, and peace in all we do. Amen.

Day 17

Holy Reverence

Reading: Leviticus 10

Leviticus 10 presents a sobering narrative: the sudden death of Aaron's sons, Nadab and Abihu, for offering "unauthorized fire" before the Lord. This event starkly illustrates the seriousness with which God views the holiness of worship and obedience to divine commands. Through this account, we are invited to reflect on the profound respect and reverence due to God in our worship and lives.

This chapter underscores a fundamental principle: we should not approach God's holiness casually or presumptuously. Nadab and Abihu's actions, whether through thoughtlessness or arrogance, represent a departure from God's explicit instructions. Their tragic end is a potent reminder of the weight of our call to worship God in spirit and truth, adhering closely to divine guidance.

Leviticus 10 speaks volumes about the nature of our approach to God. It calls us to a posture of humility and obedience, recognizing that our worship is not about personal preference or innovation but about aligning our hearts and actions with God's desires. This chapter challenges us to examine the sincerity and reverence of our worship, encouraging us to approach God with the awe and respect God deserves.

LEVITICUS

Leviticus 10 offers insights into how Christians should live, extending beyond the context of formal worship to encompass our daily lives. The principles of humility, obedience, and reverence for God's holiness are foundational to living a life that reflects God's character. As followers of Christ, we are called to embody love, justice, reconciliation, and compassion, not as abstract ideals but as concrete expressions of our reverence for God. Our faith should motivate us to act justly, love mercy, and walk humbly with our God, engaging in acts of service and forgiveness that mirror the heart of God for humanity and creation.

In the light of the New Testament, Leviticus 10 points us to Jesus, who perfectly embodies obedience, reverence, and the fulfillment of worship. Through his life, death, and resurrection, Jesus demonstrates how to live in perfect harmony with God's will, offering himself as the ultimate sacrifice for our sins. In Christ, we find the example and the empowerment to pursue lives pleasing to God, marked by the Spirit's fruit of love, joy, peace, patience, kindness, goodness, faithfulness, gentleness, and self-control.

Big Idea: Approach God with reverence and live out divine commands humbly, reflecting Christ's obedience and love.

Reflection: How does my worship and approach to daily living reflect a deep reverence for God's holiness? How can I more fully embody the humility, obedience, and love that Jesus exemplifies?

Prayer: Heavenly Parent, we stand in awe of your holiness and righteousness. Teach us to approach you with the reverence and humility that you deserve. Help us to live in a way that reflects your character, guided by your Spirit, to embody love, justice, and compassion in all we do. May our worship and lives be pleasing in your sight as we seek to follow the example of your Son, Jesus Christ. Amen.

Day 18

Holiness in Everyday Choices

Reading: Leviticus 11

Leviticus 11 is a detailed exposition of dietary laws, delineating clean and unclean animals and setting forth guidelines for what the Israelites were permitted to eat. These regulations, far from being mere ancient dietary restrictions, symbolize a deeper spiritual reality. They were designed to set God's people apart, reminding them of their distinct identity and calling in a world where such distinctions were often blurred.

The essence of Leviticus 11 lies in its call to holiness. God's instructions about clean and unclean foods are a tangible expression of the holiness God desires in all aspects of life. This chapter is not just about food; it's about living a life that reflects God's purity and being mindful of the influences we allow into our lives, whether physical, moral, or spiritual.

Leviticus 11 invites us to consider what it means to be set apart for God. Just as God called the Israelites to distinguish between the clean and unclean, the Spirit calls us to discernment in our spiritual walk. This discernment applies to our choices, relationships, and even the thoughts we entertain, challenging us to live in a manner that honors God and reflects the divine character to those around us.

Leviticus

In the broader context of Christian living, Leviticus 11 speaks to themes of peace, justice, reconciliation, love, humility, service, faith, compassion, and forgiveness. These themes are not disconnected from the concept of holiness; instead, they are expressions of a life set apart for God. Living out these values in our daily lives reveals the transforming power of God's Spirit within us, enabling us to make choices that promote peace, act justly, offer forgiveness, and serve others in love and humility. Our commitment to these principles is a beacon of light in a world often characterized by division and selfishness.

The dietary laws of Leviticus 11 remind us of Jesus, the one who fulfilled the Law and opened a new way of understanding holiness. In Christ, the distinctions between clean and unclean are transcended, inviting all into a relationship with God based on grace rather than adherence to specific dietary codes. Jesus's life, teachings, and sacrifice embody the ultimate expression of holiness, love, and service, offering us a model for how to live in response to God's call.

Big Idea: Live set apart for God, embodying holiness through choices that reflect God's love and grace in every aspect of life.

Reflection: How does my life reflect a commitment to holiness in my everyday choices? In what ways am I living out the values of peace, justice, love, and service as an expression of my faith in Jesus?

Prayer: Holy God, who calls us to be set apart for your purposes, grant us the wisdom to discern your will in every aspect of our lives. Help us to embody the holiness, love, and compassion of Jesus in our actions and relationships. Strengthen us by your Spirit to live in a way that honors you and draws others closer to your grace. Amen.

Day 19

Sacred Moments of Grace

Reading: Leviticus 12

Leviticus 12 considers the purification process for women following childbirth, prescribing a period of separation, and concludes with offerings for purification. This chapter, while deeply rooted in the Levitical context, transcends its immediate setting to speak to themes of purity, community, and the sanctity of life. It reflects a holistic understanding of the human experience, acknowledging the joy of new life and the necessity of approaching God with reverence.

The biblical meaning of Leviticus 12 centers on recognizing human frailty and providing grace through prescribed rituals. These practices underscore the importance of both physical and spiritual cleanliness, reinforcing the community's ongoing relationship with God. This chapter is not merely about ritual compliance but the deeper reality of God's holiness and our call to live in a manner that honors that holiness.

For our spiritual lives, Leviticus 12 invites us to reflect on how we recognize and honor the sacredness in all aspects of life, including those as natural and joyful as childbirth. It challenges us to consider how we, too, might need periods of rest, reflection, and renewal in our walks with God. This passage encourages us to embrace practices that draw us closer to God, acknowledging our dependence on divine grace for purification and holiness.

Leviticus 12 also informs how Christians should live, particularly in terms of embracing and practicing values such as peace, justice, reconciliation, and compassion. In a broader sense, it calls us to recognize the sanctity of life and the importance of community support in times of joy and vulnerability. As followers of Christ, we are encouraged to extend grace and support to those around us, recognizing the various seasons of life and the different ways people may seek to draw closer to God.

Jesus is the embodiment of purity and the one who fulfills all requirements for holiness on our behalf. In Christ, purification rituals are completed, as he offers himself as the perfect sacrifice, ensuring that all who come to him are made clean. Jesus's love, presence, Spirit, and grace enable us to live out the true spirit of the laws in Leviticus, moving beyond the external acts to the heart of worship and community life rooted in love and grace.

Big Idea: Embrace and honor life's sacred moments with grace, drawing closer to God and community through Jesus's perfect purification.

Reflection: How do I honor the sacred moments in life as opportunities for drawing closer to God? How can I offer support and grace to those in my community experiencing times of joy or purification?

Prayer: Gracious God, who sanctifies us through your love and grace, teach us to recognize and honor the sacredness of every moment you grant us. Help us to support one another in love, reflecting your grace in our communities. May we find our purification and holiness in Jesus Christ, through whom we are made whole. Amen.

Day 20

Compassion beyond Borders

Reading: Leviticus 13:1-46

Leviticus 13:1-46 meticulously details the laws regarding skin diseases, often broadly termed as leprosy, outlining the procedures for diagnosis and the rituals for those found unclean. This passage, while deeply rooted in ancient health practices and theological purity codes, speaks volumes about the nature of community, cleanliness, and the compassionate heart of God towards those suffering and marginalized.

The biblical meaning of these verses extends beyond the physical ailments to symbolize the deeper spiritual maladies that affect humanity. The meticulous examination by priests reflects God's concern for purity within the community, not just as an end in itself but as a means to restore people to full community life and worship. This attention to detail in identifying and managing impurity underscores a profound understanding of holiness, suggesting that spiritual health and community integrity are intertwined.

For our spiritual lives, Leviticus 13:1-46 prompts a reflection on how we deal with spiritual "uncleanliness" or sin. Just as the priests played a role in diagnosing and restoring the unclean, we are invited into a process of self-examination and repentance, seeking restoration with God and our community. This passage encourages us to approach our spiritual condition with honesty and humility, recognizing our need for God's cleansing and healing grace.

These verses inform how Christians should live, particularly in responding to the marginalized and those suffering. The isolation experienced by those with leprosy in ancient times mirrors the exclusion often felt by those deemed "unclean" or "unworthy" by church and society today. As followers of Christ, we are called to embody his love, inclusion, hospitality, and compassion, reaching out to those on the fringes and offering hope and tangible support. This includes pursuing justice, practicing reconciliation, and showing unconditional love, reflecting Jesus's ministry to the lepers, the outcasts, and the sinners.

Jesus is the one who touched and loved those whom society and religious institutions considered untouchable and unlovable. As recorded in the Gospels, Jesus's interactions with lepers reveal his heart for healing and restoration, both physically, spiritually, and socially. In Christ, we find the ultimate expression of God's desire for purity and wholeness among all people and creation. Jesus's life, death, and resurrection offer the ultimate cleansing from sin, inviting us into a new life marked by grace, love, and community.

Big Idea: Adopt and extend Jesus's compassion by actively seeking to heal, include, and restore those marginalized by society.

Reflection: How do we respond to the "lepers" in our midst today? Are we agents of healing and inclusion, reflecting the love and compassion of Jesus?

Prayer: Gracious God, who heals the sick and restores the outcast, help us to see with your eyes and love with your heart. Guide us to be instruments of your healing and reconciliation in a broken world. May we embody the compassion and grace of Jesus, reaching out to those in need with open arms. Cleanse us from all unrighteousness and renew us in your love, that we might live as faithful disciples, reflecting your kingdom here on earth. Amen.

Day 21

Garments of Grace

Reading: Leviticus 13:47-59

In Leviticus 13:47-59, we are presented with a detailed description of how to deal with mold contamination in garments. At first glance, this passage may seem distant and unrelated to our modern spiritual sojourn. However, deeper reflection reveals profound insights into the nature of purity, community responsibility, and our relationship with the Divine.

The text meticulously outlines the process for identifying and responding to contamination, emphasizing a communal approach to addressing impurity. This process underscores a crucial biblical principle: the pursuit of holiness is not merely a personal endeavor but a collective responsibility. It invites us to consider how we, as a community of faith, respond to the metaphorical "contaminations" in our midst—be they sin, injustice, or brokenness.

This passage indicates the need for discernment and purification in our spiritual lives. Just as the priests examined garments for contamination, we are called to examine our hearts and communities for anything that might separate us from God's holiness. This examination is not for condemnation but for restoration and reconciliation.

Leviticus

In a world marred by division and strife, Leviticus 13:47–59 challenges us to embrace peace, justice, and reconciliation practices. It calls us to a life of humility, service, and compassion, reflecting God's love for those around us. This passage encourages us to seek and extend forgiveness, to love our neighbors and enemies, mirroring God's inclusive and reconciling heart.

At the heart of this message is Jesus Christ, who embodies and fulfills the profound themes of this Levitical text. In Jesus, we see the ultimate expression of purity, not through separation but through embracing our brokenness. His life, death, and resurrection demonstrate how divine love transforms and restores, offering us a new identity as beloved children of God. Through Jesus's presence, spirit, and grace, we are empowered to live out the high calling of discipleship, responding to the challenges and opportunities presented in Leviticus 13:47–59.

Big Idea: Seek community-focused purity through Jesus's grace, leading to reconciliation and holistic transformation.

Reflection: How are we called to be agents of purification and reconciliation in our communities? And how does Jesus's example inspire us to engage with the "contaminations" of our world with compassion and grace?

Prayer: Gracious God, guide us in our pilgrimage towards holiness, not as a path of isolation, but as a call to community, service, and love. Help us see Jesus's presence in every aspect of our lives, empowering us to live out the lessons of Leviticus with compassion and humility. May your Spirit lead us into deeper understanding and faithfulness as we seek to embody your love and grace to those around us. Amen.

Day 22

Restoration's Call

Reading: Leviticus 14:1-32

In Leviticus 14:1-32, we are given a rich and detailed account of the rituals for cleansing from skin diseases, a process of physical healing, spiritual restoration, and reintegration into the community. This passage, with its intricate ceremonies involving sacrifice, washing, and anointing, speaks volumes about purity, forgiveness, and restoring relationships with God and within the community.

At its core, this Scripture underscores the transformative power of grace and redemption. The rituals, which might seem distant and archaic, symbolize a more profound, universal truth: the path to restoration requires acknowledgment of our impurities, a willingness to undergo a cleansing process, and an acceptance of divine grace. These steps towards healing mirror our spiritual pilgrimage highlighting the necessity of confronting our brokenness, seeking forgiveness, and embracing the renewal offered through God's love.

The principles outlined in Leviticus 14:1-32 inform how Christians are called to live in profound ways. They encourage us to pursue peace, practice justice, and engage in acts of reconciliation and love. This passage calls us to a life marked by humility, service, and compassion, reflecting the heart of a God who seeks to cleanse, restore, and reconcile. It reminds us that our faith is not a private affair but a communal journey, where forgiveness and loving our neighbors and enemies are central to our witness in the world.

In the light of the New Testament, Jesus Christ embodies and fulfills these Levitical rituals of cleansing and restoration. Through his life, death, and resurrection, Jesus has made the ultimate sacrifice, offering himself to cleanse us from our sins and restore our relationship with God. His ministry was marked by acts of healing and reconciliation, breaking down barriers and inviting all into a new life of freedom and grace. As followers of Christ, we are empowered by his Spirit to live out these themes of Leviticus, serving as agents of healing, peace, and reconciliation in a broken world.

Big Idea: Live as restored agents of grace, embodying Christ's healing and reconciliation in every relationship.

Reflection: How does the process of cleansing and restoration in Leviticus 14:1–32 mirror our spiritual journey? And how can we, empowered by Jesus's example and the Holy Spirit, be instruments of peace and reconciliation in our communities?

Prayer: Healing and reconciling God, guide us through our processes of cleansing and restoration, drawing us closer to you and each other. Help us live out Leviticus's lessons, embodying your grace, love, and compassion. Empower us by your Spirit to be beacons of light in a world needing healing and reconciliation. In Jesus's name, we pray. Amen.

Day 23

Sanctified Spaces

Reading: Leviticus 14:33-57

In the latter half of Leviticus 14, the Scripture focuses on the purification of houses afflicted with what might be described as mold or leprosy. While seemingly focused on the physical, this passage carries profound spiritual and theological implications. It speaks to the reality of contamination—not just of individual lives but of the spaces we inhabit together. This text invites us to see our communities and shared environments as places needing God's cleansing and restoration.

This section of Leviticus teaches us about the communal nature of sin and purity. Just as the physical spaces we share can become contaminated and require purification, so too can the spiritual and relational environments of our communities. It underscores the importance of vigilance and responsibility in maintaining the sanctity of our communal life. The process of cleansing a house, with its detailed rituals, reflects a profound truth: purification and reconciliation require intentional, deliberate actions.

The principles outlined in Leviticus 14:33-57 offer a blueprint for how Christians might live out their faith in a world marred by sin and brokenness. They call us to a life of peace, justice, and reconciliation, urging us to take seriously our role as stewards of our communities and the wider world. This passage encourages us to act with love, humility, service, and compassion, actively working to cleanse and heal our environments. It challenges us to extend forgiveness, love our neighbors and enemies, and pursue a life marked by faith and the quest for purity—personally and collectively.

In Jesus Christ, we see the ultimate fulfillment of these Levitical laws. Jesus embodies the perfect priest who identifies the contamination of sin and provides the ultimate means for our cleansing through his sacrifice on the cross. His ministry, characterized by healing, teaching, and reconciling work, illustrates how divine love transforms and restores. Through Christ's love, presence, spirit, and grace, we are empowered to live as his disciples, responding to the challenges of contamination in our lives and communities with hope and action.

Big Idea: Cultivate communal purity and restoration, reflecting Christ's transformative love in every shared space.

Reflection: How do we contribute to the purity and health of our communal spaces? How does the example of Jesus inspire us to pursue reconciliation and healing within our communities?

Prayer: Healing God, grant us the wisdom and strength to be vigilant stewards of the places you have entrusted to us. Help us see our communities through your eyes—spaces needing your cleansing and healing touch. Empower us by your Spirit to live out the lessons of Leviticus, embodying your love and grace in every action through Jesus Christ, our Lord. Amen.

Day 24

Grace-Enabled Purification

Reading: Leviticus 15

Leviticus 15 is about the laws regarding bodily discharges, outlining measures for handling what was considered unclean and detailing the rituals for purification. While these prescriptions may initially appear distant from our contemporary spiritual lives they offer profound insights into concepts of purity, community health, and our approach to the sacred.

This chapter reminds us of the intrinsic connection between physical cleanliness and spiritual holiness in ancient Israelite society, emphasizing the importance of maintaining purity within the community. These regulations, far from being mere ancient health codes, symbolize the deeper reality of sin's impact on our lives and relationships and the necessity of purification to restore fellowship with God and one another.

Leviticus 15 speaks to our spiritual lives by highlighting the need for awareness and confession of our physical, spiritual, or relational impurities. Just as the Israelites were called to acknowledge their unclean state and undergo a process of cleansing, we, too, are invited to recognize our imperfections and seek God's grace for purification. This passage challenges us to consider how

Leviticus

sin separates us from God and others and the lengths to which God goes to restore us.

Regarding how Christians are called to live, Leviticus 15 encourages practices of humility, compassion, and a commitment to community welfare. It teaches us to be mindful of how our actions and conditions affect those around us, urging a lifestyle prioritizing peace, justice, and reconciliation. The passage invites us to reflect on our need for cleansing and to extend grace and forgiveness to others, recognizing that we all need God's mercy.

Jesus Christ, in his ministry, fulfilled and transcended these Levitical laws by offering himself as the ultimate source of purification. Through his sacrifice, we are cleansed from our sins and restored to a right relationship with God. Jesus embodies the compassionate healer, touching and healing those considered untouchable, breaking down barriers of impurity, and inviting all into a new life of holiness and grace. His example inspires us to live out our faith with love, serving as agents of healing and reconciliation in a broken world.

Big Idea: Embrace and extend God's cleansing grace to foster purity, healing, and unity within our communities.

Reflection: How do we respond to our imperfections and those of others? Are we willing to seek and offer the grace needed for cleansing and restoration?

Prayer: Our God who cleanses and restores, please teach us to walk in humility and purity, mindful of our need for your cleansing grace. Help us to live in a manner that honors you and edifies our community, following the example of Jesus, who makes all things new. Empower us by your Spirit to be agents of healing and reconciliation, embodying your love in every aspect of our lives. Amen.

Day 25

Living Atonement

Reading: Leviticus 16

Leviticus 16 describes the Day of Atonement, Yom Kippur, a sacred time of communal purification and reconciliation with God. On this day, through elaborate rituals, the high priest made atonement for the people's sins, symbolically transferring them to a scapegoat sent into the wilderness. This chapter, rich with symbolism, offers profound insights into sin, forgiveness, and how a holy God makes provision for the reconciliation of people.

The Day of Atonement underscores the seriousness with which God views sin and the lengths God will go to restore fellowship with humanity and all creation. It emphasizes the need for personal and communal confession and repentance, highlighting the importance of a mediator in the reconciliation process. This ancient observance invites us to reflect on the nature of atonement, the cost of sin, and God's incredible mercy, providing a way for purification and restoration.

For our spiritual lives, Leviticus 16 points to the deep need for atonement that none of us can achieve on our own. It reminds us of the gravity of our sin and the profound need for a Savior who can bridge the gap between humanity and the Divine. This passage calls us to a posture of humility, recognizing our utter dependence on God's grace for our cleansing and forgiveness.

Considering Leviticus 16, Christians are called to nurture lives marked by peace, justice, and reconciliation. Understanding the depth of forgiveness we have received through Christ, we are empowered to extend forgiveness to others, actively seeking to repair broken relationships and foster unity within our communities. This chapter challenges us to live out our faith with compassion, serving others and loving our neighbors and enemies as tangible expressions of the atonement we have experienced in Christ.

Jesus, fulfilling the Day of Atonement, embodies the ultimate high priest who makes atonement for our sins and becomes the atoning sacrifice himself. Through his death and resurrection, Jesus accomplishes what the rituals of Leviticus 16 could only symbolize: the complete removal of our sins and the restoration of our relationship with God. In Christ, we find the true and living way to approach God, not with fear, but with confidence in God's mercy and grace.

Big Idea: Embody Christ's atoning love by extending forgiveness and fostering reconciliation in every relationship.

Reflection: How does understanding the depth of God's forgiveness through Christ move us to forgive and seek reconciliation with others? How can we live as reflections of God's atoning love in our communities?

Prayer: Forgiving and reconciling God, we thank you for the gift of atonement, made once and for all through Jesus Christ. Teach us to grasp the depth of your forgiveness so that we might extend grace to others with humility and love. Fill us with your Spirit, that we may live as agents of reconciliation, embodying the peace and justice of your kingdom. In Jesus's name, amen.

Day 26

Anchored in the Sacred

Reading: Leviticus 17

Leviticus 17 is a pivotal chapter in the biblical narrative, emphasizing the sanctity of blood and its exclusive use in the sacrificial system ordained by God. This chapter commands that all slaughter of animals, whether for sacrifice or food, must occur at the tabernacle, underscoring that life, represented by blood, belongs solely to God. This directive sought to centralize worship, prevent idolatry, and instill a deep respect for life and the divine provision for atonement.

For our spiritual lives, Leviticus 17 is a profound reminder of the cost of sin and the preciousness of life. It teaches us that life is not ours to take casually or capriciously but is a sacred gift from God, with its redemption rooted in divine grace. The regulations about blood underscore a theological truth central to both the Old and New Testaments: without the shedding of blood, there is no forgiveness of sins. This principle points us towards a posture of humility and gratitude, recognizing our dependence on God's provision for atonement.

Considering Leviticus 17, Christians are called to live with a heightened sense of the sanctity of life and the seriousness of sin. This awareness should lead us to pursue peace, act justly, and live out our reconciliation with God in ways that reflect God's love, mercy, and forgiveness. The chapter challenges us to embody the values of the kingdom of God, promoting life, engaging in humble service, and extending compassion to all. It encourages us to view our relationships and our stewardship of life through the lens of God's overarching love and redemption plan, fostering communities where love, forgiveness, and neighborly kindness prevail.

Jesus, the fulfillment of the sacrificial system, embodies and surpasses the teachings of Leviticus 17. Through his death on the cross, Jesus becomes the ultimate sacrifice—his blood shed for the forgiveness of sins for all who believe. In Christ, the sanctity of life and the gravity of sin meet God's boundless mercy and love. As followers of Christ, we are empowered by his Spirit to live in a way that honors his sacrifice, reflecting his love and grace in our daily lives and interactions.

Big Idea: Anchor your life in Christ, honoring God as the source of life and sustainer of all relationships.

Reflection: How does the sanctity of life shape our actions and attitudes towards others? How does the ultimate sacrifice of Jesus inspire us to lead lives marked by forgiveness, service, and love?

Prayer: Gracious God, thank you for the gift of life and the provision of redemption through the blood of Jesus. Teach us to treasure life's sanctity and live in the light of your grace, embodying your love and forgiveness in all we do. Help us to be agents of reconciliation and peace, reflecting the sacrifice of Jesus in our words and actions. Amen.

Day 27

Holy Reflections

Reading: Leviticus 18

Leviticus 18 stands as a pivotal chapter in the Levitical law, delineating boundaries around sexual conduct and relationships. It articulates a vision for holiness in personal and communal life, distinguishing the people of Israel from the practices of surrounding nations. This chapter is not merely about prohibition but about forming a community that reflects God's holiness and intention for human relationships.

The text invites us to reflect on the broader implications of living in ways that honor God's design for life and relationships. It challenges us to consider how our personal choices affect our community, urging us towards a life marked by purity, integrity, and respect for the dignity of all persons. This call to holiness is as relevant today as it was in ancient times, reminding us that our relationships with others reflect our relationship with God.

For our spiritual lives, Leviticus 18 encourages us to deeply consider the boundaries we set and how we honor God and others through our choices. It prompts a reflection on the nature of holiness, not as an abstract concept but as a lived reality that influences every aspect of our lives. This chapter invites us to live in a countercultural manner, not for the sake of being different, but to bear witness to God's life-giving and liberating ways.

Regarding how Christians are called to live, Leviticus 18 points to principles of justice, love, and reconciliation. It calls us to be people of peace, living out our faith with humility and service, and embodying compassion and forgiveness in our relationships. This passage urges us to love our neighbors, including our enemies, as a tangible expression of our love for God. It challenges us to consider how our actions, especially in the most intimate areas of life, contribute to the flourishing or the hurting of others.

Jesus Christ, in his life and teachings, embodies and fulfills the holiness to which Leviticus 18 calls us. We are empowered to live out these challenging teachings through his love, presence, spirit, and grace. Jesus models a way of love that honors the Father, showing us that true holiness is found in loving God and others. In Christ, we find the strength and grace to lead lives that reflect God's holiness in our relationships and communities.

Big Idea: Live in holiness that reflects God's love and transforms relationships through Christ's grace.

Reflection: How do our choices and relationships reflect God's holiness? How can we, through the power of Christ's love and the Spirit, pursue lives that honor God and bring healing and wholeness to our communities?

Prayer: Transforming and loving God, please guide us in your ways of holiness, teaching us to honor you in all our relationships. Help us to lead lives that reflect your love and purity, empowered by the grace of your Son, Jesus Christ. May your Spirit guide us in truth and love, enabling us to be agents of healing and reconciliation in a broken world. Amen.

Day 28

Devoted to Holiness

Reading: Leviticus 19:1-8

Leviticus 19:1-8 calls the people of Israel to holiness, emphasizing the need for pure worship and a life dedicated to God. This section of Scripture is not just about ritual purity but speaks to the integrity of one's relationship with God, manifested in obedience and respect for God's commandments. The sacrifices mentioned are to be offered in a spirit of devotion, not merely as a formality but as an expression of a heart wholly committed to God.

This passage challenges us to examine the authenticity of our worship and the depth of our commitment to God. It prompts us to reflect on how our spiritual practices and daily lives align with God's call to holiness. Just as the Israelites were instructed to bring their offerings with a sincere heart, we are called to approach God with genuine devotion, ensuring that our worship is not just a ritual but a true reflection of our reverence for God.

In the broader context of Christian living, Leviticus 19:1-8 invites us to consider how our actions and choices reflect our commitment to God and divine commandments. It encourages us to seek lives characterized by peace, justice, and love, embodying the holiness to which God calls us. This passage reminds us that our worship of God is intimately connected with our ethical behavior, urging us to treat others compassionately, act justly, and walk humbly with God. It calls us to a life of service, where forgiveness and loving our neighbors and enemies are expressions of our worship and devotion to God.

Jesus, the embodiment of God's love and grace, perfectly fulfills the holiness that Leviticus 19:1–8 demands. We see the ultimate example of pure worship and dedicated service to God in him. Jesus's life, teachings, and sacrifice on the cross provide how we can live out the call to holiness. Through Christ's presence and spirit, we are empowered to pursue justice, love mercy, and walk humbly with our God, reflecting his love in our relationships and actions.

Big Idea: Embrace genuine worship and ethical living as expressions of our devotion to God's holiness.

Reflection: How does our worship reflect our commitment to God's holiness? How can we, empowered by Jesus's example, live out this call to holiness in our daily lives?

Prayer: Holy and ethical God, instill in us a heart of true devotion so that our worship may reflect our genuine commitment to your holiness. Guide us by your Spirit to live in a way that honors you in all we do, following the example of your Son, Jesus Christ. Help us to embody your love and grace in our actions and relationships, serving as beacons of your light in a world in need. Amen.

Day 29

Holiness in Action

Reading: Leviticus 19:9-29

Leviticus 19:9-29 presents laws to foster a community characterized by justice, generosity, and holiness. From the command to leave gleanings for the poor to prohibitions against dishonesty and injustice, this passage nurtures the ethical imagination of Israelite society, grounding it in the character of God. It challenges the community to reflect God's holiness in every aspect of life, from economic practices to personal relationships.

This section of Leviticus is not merely a collection of ancient rules but a timeless call to live out our faith in practical, tangible ways. It reminds us that our spiritual lives are inseparable from our actions and interactions. In this passage, the command to love our neighbor as ourselves encapsulates the essence of God's law and reveals the heart of what it means to follow God. It calls us to a life marked by compassion, justice, and a commitment to the well-being of others, especially the most vulnerable among us.

For Christians today, Leviticus 19:9-29 is a profound reminder that our faith must be lived out in the community context, where love, justice, and mercy are not abstract concepts but daily realities. It challenges us to examine how we treat others, conduct our business, and steward the resources God has entrusted us. This passage invites us to be agents of reconciliation, to pursue peace, act with humility and integrity, and embody Christ's love and compassion in every facet of our lives.

Jesus Christ is the perfect embodiment of the principles outlined in Leviticus 19. His life and ministry demonstrated what it truly means to love God and our neighbor. Through his teachings, actions, and sacrifice on the cross, Jesus showed us the depth of God's love and the way to true holiness. By his grace, we are empowered to live according to these high standards, reflecting his love to a world in need.

Big Idea: Reflect God's holiness in daily life through acts of justice, generosity, and compassion.

Reflection: How does our life reflect God's call to justice, generosity, and holiness? How can we, empowered by the spirit of Christ, be a source of blessing to our community?

Prayer: Generous and compassionate God, instill in us a heart that mirrors your love and holiness. Guide us to live out the teachings of Leviticus 19, loving our neighbors and serving the vulnerable among us. Help us to embody the justice, generosity, and compassion of Jesus in all that we do so that our lives may glorify you and bring your light to those around us. Amen.

Day 30

Integrity of Holiness

Reading: Leviticus 19:30-37

Leviticus 19:30-37 guides the Israelites in living a life that honors God, focusing on the sanctity of Sabbaths, reverence for the sanctuary, and integrity in personal dealings. These verses emphasize the importance of worship, fair dealings, and honest measures in every aspect of life. This passage, rich in its call to holiness, reminds the people of their unique relationship with God and the practical outworking of that relationship in everyday life.

For our spiritual lives, this section of Leviticus teaches us about integrating faith and practice. It challenges us to consider how our worship of God and daily interactions reflect our commitment to living according to divine principles. The call to keep Sabbaths holy is to rest in God's provision and sovereignty, acknowledging God as the source of all blessings. The emphasis on honesty and fairness in dealings reflects God's justice, urging us to embody these divine attributes in our relationships with others.

In the broader Christian life, Leviticus 19:30-37 informs us that our faith is not confined to personal piety or religious observances alone but is demonstrated in our ethical behavior and social interactions. This passage invites us to live out our faith with integrity, ensuring that our actions towards others reflect God's love and justice. It calls us to be agents of reconciliation, peace, and justice, embodying Christ's love in a world often marred by injustice and deceit. By living according to these precepts, we bear witness to the gospel's transformative power, which calls us to a higher standard of living.

Jesus Christ fulfills the law, including the ethical and ceremonial laws outlined in Leviticus. We see the perfect example of holiness, integrity, and love in him. Through his teachings, death, and resurrection, Jesus embodies the principles of Leviticus, showing us how to live in a relationship with God and one another. His life demonstrates the importance of worship, rest, honesty, and justice, empowering us by his Spirit to live out these values daily.

Big Idea: Live with integrity, reflecting God's holiness in worship and every aspect of daily life.

Reflection: How do our worship and daily practices reflect our commitment to God's holiness? How can we embody the principles of justice, honesty, and integrity in our community through Christ's love and Spirit?

Prayer: Gracious God, help us to honor you in our worship and our daily lives, living out the principles of honesty, integrity, and justice. May our lives reflect your holiness and love, guided by the example of Jesus Christ. Empower us by your Spirit to be faithful witnesses of your kingdom in every word we speak and action we take. Amen.

Day 31

Living Holiness

Reading: Leviticus 20:1-21

In the heart of Leviticus, nestled amid commands and decrees, lies a profound call to holiness. Leviticus 20:1–21 moves us to lives set apart, not merely in ritual but in ethical practice and spiritual devotion. This passage, with its stern warnings against practices that degrade life and community, speaks volumes about the sanctity of life, the importance of community, and the depth of God's desire for a people marked by holiness.

At first glance, these verses may seem distant, rooted in a context far removed from our modern sensibilities. Yet, they beckon us to understand a deeper truth: our actions and choices have spiritual ramifications that ripple through our lives and communities. The call to holiness is as relevant today as it was then, asking us to consider how we live in relation to God, one another, and the world around us.

The essence of Leviticus 20 is not merely about adherence to a set of rules; it's about embodying a posture of the heart that aligns with God's character. This alignment brings into sharp focus the ideals of peace, justice, and reconciliation. It challenges us to love our neighbors, act compassionately, and serve humbly. In this light, our spiritual lives are not compartmentalized segments of worship and piety but are integrated into every interaction, every decision, and every moment of our daily lives.

How, then, does this ancient text inform how we should live as followers of Christ today? It calls us to a radical way of living, reflecting God's holiness through love, service, and forgiveness. This way of life doesn't ignore justice; it embodies it, ensuring that our communities are places where everyone is valued, and dignity is upheld. In pursuing holiness, we find the essence of peace and reconciliation—not as lofty ideals but as tangible realities forged in the crucible of daily living.

The person of Jesus Christ embodies the perfect response to the themes of Leviticus 20. We see the culmination of love, service, and sacrifice in Jesus. Through his life and teachings, Jesus illustrates how to live out these ancient commands in a way that is not only relevant but transformative. His love empowers us, his presence guides us, and his Spirit enables us to nurture lives that reflect God's holiness in our complex and often broken world.

Big Idea: Cherish a life of radical holiness through love, justice, and service, reflecting God's character in every action.

Reflection: How does your life reflect God's call to holiness? How can you embody peace, justice, and reconciliation in your community?

Prayer: O God, who calls us to a life of holiness and service, empower us by your Spirit to live out your commands with love and grace. Help us to see your face in those around us, especially the least of these, and to serve them as we would serve you. In the name of Jesus Christ, who shows us the way, amen.

Day 32

Distinct for Holiness

Reading: Leviticus 20:22-27

In the closing verses of Leviticus 20, we are presented with a powerful call to distinctiveness and holiness. This passage is not merely an ancient text with outdated instructions; it is an animated, living call to God's people to embody a radical otherness in a world that often blurs the lines between sacred and secular. The command to "be holy because I am holy" is a directive that transcends time, urging us to lead lives that reflect the character of God in every aspect.

What does it mean for us today to heed this call to holiness and separation? It's about more than just avoiding certain behaviors or conforming to a set of external rules. It's about cultivating an inner transformation that affects how we live, love, and interact with the world. This transformation is rooted in the love and grace that God extends to us, empowering us to extend that same love and grace to others. It's about living in such a way that our lives point beyond ourselves to the God who calls us to be different.

Living out the principles in Leviticus 20:22-27 means embracing a lifestyle marked by peace, justice, and reconciliation. It involves loving our neighbors and enemies, showing compassion to the marginalized, serving humbly, and forgiving as we have been forgiven. These are not optional add-ons to the Christian life but are essential markers of a life transformed by God's Spirit.

In Jesus, we see the perfect embodiment of holiness and distinctiveness. He lived entirely in the world, yet not of it, engaging with those around him in ways that consistently reflected God's character. Through his teachings, actions, and ultimate sacrifice on the cross, Jesus demonstrated what it means to be set apart for God's purposes. He invites us to follow in his footsteps, empowered by his Spirit, to lead lives that reflect his love and grace to a watching world.

Big Idea: Live distinctly in God's holiness, embodying God's love, justice, and grace in every aspect of life.

Reflection: How does your life reflect the holiness to which God calls you? How can you live more distinctly for God in your everyday interactions?

Prayer: Gracious God, who calls us to be holy as you are holy, guide us by your Spirit to pursue lives that reflect your love and grace. Please help us to embody peace, justice, and reconciliation in our actions and relationships. May our lives point others to you, the source of our strength and hope. In the name of Jesus, who shows us the way, amen.

Day 33

Holiness in Practice

Reading: Leviticus 21:1–22:16

In the heart of Leviticus, chapters 21 and 22 extend a profound invitation to holiness and purity for the priests of ancient Israel and all who seek to approach the Divine. These passages delineate a series of regulations for the priests, emphasizing the importance of purity in their personal lives and their service to God. The call to holiness is clear: those who serve God must reflect God's holiness in every aspect of their lives.

What does this ancient call mean for us today? It beckons us to consider our own lives as offerings to God, reminding us that our daily actions, thoughts, and attitudes should mirror the holiness of God. This is not a call to perfection but intentionality in how we live out our faith in a world that often seems at odds with the values of the kingdom of God. It's about living so that our very lives testify to the grace and love extended to us.

The principles found in Leviticus 21 and 22 guide us towards a life of integrity, where our internal convictions match our outward actions. This integrity fosters peace, nurtures justice, and cultivates reconciliation in our relationships and communities. It challenges us to love deeply, serve humbly, and extend forgiveness generously, mirroring the compassion and mercy that God shows us. These are not mere ideals but tangible expressions of our faith, lived out in the mundane moments of everyday life.

In Jesus, we find the perfect embodiment of the holiness to which Leviticus calls God's people. Jesus lived a life of perfect purity, not as an unattainable standard, but as a demonstration of what it means to be fully devoted to God. Jesus bridged the gap between our imperfections and God's holiness through his life, death, and resurrection, offering us grace to walk in his ways. His Spirit empowers us to live in a way that reflects his love and holiness, enabling us to be his hands and feet in a world in desperate need of redemption.

Big Idea: Reflect God's holiness in every facet of life, embodying his grace and love through integrity and service.

Reflection: How does your life reflect the holiness of God? How can you live more fully for God in your daily interactions?

Prayer: Holy God, please guide us by your Spirit to live in a way that reflects your holiness. Help us embody your love, justice, and mercy in all we do so that our lives may be a living testimony to your grace. Empower us to serve you with integrity, following the example of your Son, Jesus Christ. Amen.

Day 34

Pure Offerings

Reading: Leviticus 22:17-33

In Leviticus 22:17-33, we find instructions about offerings made to God, emphasizing the need for them to be without blemish, symbolizing the purity and perfection that is due to God. This passage teaches us about the seriousness with which we should approach God, offering our sacrifices and our very lives in a manner that honors Jesus Christ. It underscores the principle that our offerings, whether of time, resources, or talents, are to be given thoughtfully and concerning the holiness of the One to whom we give.

This portion of Scripture invites us to reflect on the nature of our offerings to God in our spiritual lives. It challenges us to consider the quality of our worship, devotion, and obedience. Are they "without blemish"? Do they reflect a heart fully committed to honoring God in all things? This is not about striving for unattainable perfection but about offering our best to God, recognizing that our best is made possible through the grace and mercy God in Christ extends to us.

Leviticus 22:17-33 speaks to the quality of our offerings and the inclusivity of God's covenant. It reminds us that God's promises are available to all who approach with a sincere heart, regardless of their background or past failures. This inclusivity reflects the heart of the gospel, which invites all to come to God through Jesus Christ.

In Jesus, we see the perfect sacrifice, offered once for all, fulfilling the requirements of the law and inviting us into a relationship with God based on grace, not merit. Jesus embodies the unblemished offering, and we are made clean and holy before God through Jesus. His life and ministry exemplify how we must live—offering ourselves in service, love, and worship to God and extending God's grace and love to those around us.

As Christians, we are called to live in a way that reflects the holiness of God, offering our best in all we do and extending the invitation of God's love to everyone we meet. This means pursuing peace, acting justly, loving mercy, and walking humbly with God. It means forgiving as we have been forgiven, serving with humility, and loving our neighbors—and even our enemies—with the love of Christ.

Big Idea: Offer your life as a pure and devoted sacrifice to God, reflecting divine grace and holiness in every action.

Reflection: How are you offering your life to God? Are there areas where you can offer a more "unblemished" sacrifice of your time, talents, or resources?

Prayer: Gracious God, thank you for the perfect sacrifice of your Son, Jesus, which enables us to come before you. Help us to offer our lives to you in holiness and truth, reflecting your love and grace to the world around us. May our offerings be pleasing in your sight as we live in gratitude for your mercy and grace. Amen.

Day 35

Sacred Rhythms

Reading: Leviticus 23:1-2

Leviticus 23:1-2 stands as a divine invitation to enter a rhythm of rest and celebration rooted in the sacred assemblies commanded by God. These verses are not merely an introduction to a list of festivals; they represent a call to remember, reflect, and rejoice in God's providential care and redemptive work throughout history. This passage emphasizes the importance of setting aside time from our daily routines to focus on God, acknowledging God's lordship over our time and lives.

In our relentless, fast-paced world, the message of Leviticus 23:1-2 speaks to a deep need within our souls for sabbath and celebration. It reminds us that our spiritual lives are nourished through work, service, rest, and rejoicing in God's goodness. This rhythm of rest and celebration is essential for our spiritual health, providing space for us to reflect on God's provision, recalibrate our hearts towards divine purposes, and rejuvenate our spirits through worship and fellowship with the community of believers.

Living out the principles of Leviticus 23:1-2 today means intentionally incorporating times of rest and celebration into our lives, recognizing these moments as sacred and integral to our walk with God. It challenges us to prioritize our relationship with God, setting aside time to remember God's faithfulness, to rejoice in divine grace, and to rest in Christ's presence. This practice fosters a more profound sense of peace, enriches our sense of community, and strengthens our commitment to justice, love, and service in the world around us.

Jesus embodies the fulfillment of these sacred assemblies, inviting us into the ultimate rest and celebration found in him. Through his life, death, and resurrection, Jesus has inaugurated a new covenant, offering us rest for our souls and inviting us to the eternal celebration of God's kingdom. In Jesus, we find the grace to live out the rhythms of rest and celebration, empowered by his Spirit to reflect his love and light in every aspect of our lives.

Big Idea: Nurture the divine rhythm of rest and celebration to deepen your walk with God and enrich your community.

Reflection: How are you incorporating rest and celebration into your spiritual practice? How can these rhythms deepen your relationship with God and with others?

Prayer: Creator God, teach us to embrace the rhythms of rest and celebration you have ordained. Please help us to find our rest in you and to rejoice in your goodness every day. May our lives reflect the peace and joy of your kingdom, drawing others to find their rest in you. In Jesus's name, amen.

Day 36

The Gift of Sabbath

Reading: Leviticus 23:3

Leviticus 23:3 presents the Sabbath as a day of sacred assembly and rest, a concept that, at its core, is about much more than physical cessation from labor. It's an invitation into a rhythm of life that acknowledges the sovereignty of God over our time, work, and lives. This day of rest, set apart each week, serves as a reminder that it is not our efforts that sustain the world but God's grace and provision.

The Sabbath principle speaks profoundly into our spiritual lives, calling us into a regular pattern of rest and reflection. In a culture that often values productivity over well-being, the Sabbath offers a counternarrative, teaching us that our worth is not tied to our output. It invites us to trust in God's provision, to lay down our work, and to rest in the knowledge that we are loved and valued simply because we are God's creation.

This commandment to rest, however, is for more than just our benefit. It also calls us to consider how we extend the principles of peace, justice, and compassion in our interactions with others. Observing the Sabbath challenges us to live in ways that promote rest and renewal for all of God's creation. It asks us to consider how our actions contribute to the well-being of our neighbors, encouraging us to live out the values of love, humility, and service in tangible ways.

In Jesus, we see the Sabbath fulfilled. He invites us to a more profound rest, one that is found in Christ. Jesus teaches that the Sabbath was made for humans, not humans for the Sabbath, revealing the heart of God so that God's people can find rest and renewal in Jesus. Through his life and teachings, Jesus models a life that balances work with rest, service with renewal, and activity with contemplation. His presence in our lives enables us to live out the true spirit of the Sabbath, finding our rest in him and extending his love and grace to those around us.

Big Idea: Welcome the Sabbath as a divine gift of rest, reflection, and renewal, extending peace and justice through Christ's love.

Reflection: How are you incorporating rest and reflection into your weekly rhythm? How does your observance of the Sabbath extend peace and renewal to others?

Prayer: Loving God, teach us to embrace the rest and renewal you offer us through the Sabbath. Help us to trust in your provision, to find our worth in your love, and to extend your peace and justice in the world. May our lives reflect the rest and renewal in your Son, Jesus, in whom we find our proper Sabbath rest. Amen.

Day 37

Redemptive Celebrations

Reading: Leviticus 23:4-8

Leviticus 23:4–8 introduces us to the appointed feasts of the Lord, beginning with the Passover and the Festival of Unleavened Bread. These feasts are not merely ancient rituals but profound reminders of God's deliverance and provision. They call God's people to remember God's mighty acts in history, to reflect on the Spirit's ongoing work in the world, and to rejoice in the assurance of divine presence and faithfulness.

These passages underscore the importance of remembrance, reflection, and rejoicing in our spiritual lives. They invite us to consider how God has worked in our lives and the world around us, encouraging us to cultivate a sense of gratitude and awe. This act of remembrance is not a passive recollection but an active engagement with our faith history, shaping how we understand ourselves and our place in God's ongoing story.

Living out the principles found in Leviticus 23:4–8 means embodying the themes of deliverance and provision in our daily lives. It calls us to be agents of peace, justice, and reconciliation, reflecting God's love and compassion in our interactions with others. It encourages us to serve humbly, to love generously, and to extend forgiveness, just as we have been forgiven. These festivals remind us that our faith is not a private affair but is meant to be lived out in the community, sharing in the joys and sorrows of others, and working together towards the flourishing of all.

In Jesus, we see the ultimate fulfillment of these feasts. He is our Passover lamb, whose sacrifice delivers us from sin and death and invites us into a life of freedom and joy. Jesus's life, death, and resurrection embody the themes of deliverance and provision, offering us a new way to understand and celebrate these ancient festivals. Through him, we are invited into a more profound experience of God's presence and grace, empowered to pursue lives that witness the hope and healing Jesus offers.

Big Idea: Celebrate God's redemptive acts with joyful obedience, reflecting God's love and justice in community life.

Reflection: How do you see God's deliverance and provision in your life? How can you embody the themes of these festivals in your daily interactions and relationships?

Prayer: God of redemption, thank you for the reminders of your deliverance and provision in the feasts you appointed. Please help us to remember your faithfulness, to reflect on your goodness, and to rejoice in your presence in our lives. Empower us through your Spirit to live out these truths, sharing your love and grace with the world. In the name of Jesus, our Passover Lamb. Amen.

Day 38

Firstfruits of Faith

Reading: Leviticus 23:9-14

Leviticus 23:9–14 introduces the Feast of Firstfruits, a time when the Israelites were to bring the first sheaf of their harvest to the priest, who would wave it before the Lord on their behalf. This offering was not merely agricultural protocol but a profound expression of gratitude and dependence on God. It acknowledged God as the source of all provision and blessing, recognizing that every good gift comes from above.

This passage invites us to consider the "firstfruits" of our own lives. In a spiritual sense, offering our firstfruits means dedicating the best of what we have and are to God—our time, talents, resources, and even our hearts. It's a call to prioritize our relationship with God, acknowledging God as the source of every blessing and the sustainer of our lives.

But what does this mean for our spiritual lives today? Offering our firstfruits is an act of faith and trust, demonstrating our belief that God will provide for our needs. It is also an act of worship, expressing gratitude for God's faithfulness and generosity. This practice invites us into a posture of humility and dependence on God, reminding us that we are not self-sufficient but deeply need the grace and provision of our Creator.

Living out the principle of firstfruits impacts how we engage with the world around us. It calls us to live generously, with open hands and hearts, willing to share what we have received. This generosity reflects the character of God and manifests God's love to our neighbors, promoting peace, justice, and reconciliation. Offering our firstfruits encourages us to live with a spirit of gratitude and service, recognizing that everything we have is a gift to be used for God's glory and the good of others.

In Jesus, we see the ultimate firstfruits offering. His life, death, and resurrection are the firstfruits of the new creation, the first and best offered to God on behalf of humanity. Through Jesus, we are invited into a life of sacrificial love and service, empowered by his Spirit to offer our lives as a living sacrifice, holy and pleasing to God.

Big Idea: Offer your life's firstfruits to God as an act of faith, gratitude, and dedication to God's service.

Reflection: What are the "firstfruits" of your life that you need to offer to God? How can offering your firstfruits to God shape how you live and interact with those around you?

Prayer: Generous God, thank you for the abundance you pour into our lives. Please help us to offer our firstfruits to you in a spirit of gratitude and trust, dedicating our lives to your service and glory. May our offerings reflect your love and grace to the world. In Jesus's name, amen.

Day 39

Harvest of the Spirit

Reading: Leviticus 23:15-22

Leviticus 23:15-22 describes the Feast of Weeks, also known as Pentecost, a time of thanksgiving for the harvest. This feast, coming fifty days after the Passover, is marked by the offering of new grain to the Lord, signifying the firstfruits of the harvest. It is a celebration of God's provision and faithfulness, a time for the community to unite in gratitude and worship.

This ancient observance speaks profoundly into our spiritual lives today, reminding us of the importance of recognizing and celebrating God's provision. It calls us to a posture of gratitude, acknowledging that every good gift comes from above. The Feast of Weeks encourages us to reflect on the bounty God has provided regarding physical sustenance and the spiritual nourishment we receive through God's words and the Spirit.

This feast has a profound significance for Christians today, pointing to the outpouring of the Holy Spirit at Pentecost as recorded in the Acts of the Apostles. This event marks the harvest of the firstfruits of the church, the beginning of God's new work through God's spirit among God's people. It reminds us that we are called to be a community that lives in the power of the Spirit, bearing witness to the resurrection life we have in Christ.

Leviticus

Living in the light of Leviticus 23:15–22, we are invited to embody the principles of peace, justice, reconciliation, and love daily. This passage encourages us to serve humbly, act compassionately, and extend forgiveness freely, mirroring the character of God in our interactions with others. As we celebrate God's faithfulness and provision, we are reminded to share generously with those in need, reflecting God's love and provision to a world in need.

In Jesus, we see the fulfillment of God's promise, the ultimate firstfruits offered for the world's redemption. Through his life, death, and resurrection, Jesus inaugurates a new creation, empowering us with his Spirit to live out the values of the kingdom of God. As his followers, we are called to be agents of peace, bearers of love, and workers for justice, enabled by the Spirit to bring the flavor of God's kingdom to the earth.

Big Idea: Celebrate God's provision and embody the Spirit's power in acts of service, justice, and love.

Reflection: How are you recognizing and celebrating God's provision in your life? How is the Spirit empowering you to live out Christ's kingdom values in your community?

Prayer: Gracious Lord, thank you for your provision and faithfulness. Fill us with your Spirit so we may develop lives of gratitude, generosity, and service, reflecting your love and grace to the world. Help us to bear the fruits of your Spirit, sharing your blessings with those around us. In the name of Jesus, our Redeemer, amen.

Day 40

Anticipating Faithfulness

Reading: Leviticus 23:23-25

Leviticus 23:23-25 introduces the Feast of Trumpets, a sacred time marked by rest, remembrance, and the sounding of trumpets. This day, set apart for blowing trumpets and calling the community together, is a powerful reminder of God's presence and providence. It's a call to pause, to reflect on God's faithfulness, and to reorient our hearts and lives towards God.

The Feast of Trumpets speaks to our spiritual lives by reminding us of the importance of intentional times of remembrance and celebration. Just as the Israelites were called to remember God's past acts of deliverance and provision, we, too, are invited to recall the ways God has moved in our lives. This remembrance is not passive. It requires us to actively engage with our faith, celebrating God's goodness and recommitting ourselves to God's service.

For Christians, this feast can symbolize the call to alertness and readiness for God's action in the world. It encourages us to live in anticipation, looking forward to God's work and preparing our hearts to respond in faith and obedience. This anticipation is rooted in love, humility, and a commitment to justice and peace. It challenges us to foster lives that reflect the values of God's kingdom, showing compassion to the marginalized, seeking reconciliation, and embodying God's love in our relationships.

In Jesus, we see the ultimate fulfillment of the themes of the Feast of Trumpets. Jesus embodies God's presence with us, calling us into a relationship with him and inviting us to be part of his redemptive work in the world. Through his life, teachings, and sacrifice, Jesus demonstrates how to live in anticipation of God's kingdom, showing us how to love, serve, and forgive. His Spirit empowers us to respond to God's call with joy and obedience, enabling us to live out the principles of the feast in our daily lives.

Big Idea: Live in anticipation of God's work, celebrating divine faithfulness and responding with joyful obedience.

Reflection: How are you remembering and celebrating God's faithfulness in your life? How can you live in a posture of readiness and anticipation for God's action in the world?

Prayer: Faithful God, as we remember your faithfulness and celebrate your goodness, help us live in anticipation of your work in our lives and the world. Fill us with your Spirit so we may embody your love and justice and be ready to respond to your call with faith and obedience. In the name of Jesus, who is our hope and our salvation, amen.

Day 41

Atonement in Action

Reading: Leviticus 23:26-32

In the heart of Leviticus, amid laws and rituals that may seem distant to our contemporary sensibilities, lies a profound invitation to encounter the Divine. Leviticus 23:26-32 describes the Day of Atonement as a sacred time of fasting, reflection, and reconciliation with God. This ancient observance beckons us to a deeper understanding of our spiritual journey today.

This passage not only details a ceremonial practice but also unfolds layers of spiritual truth. It reminds us of the universal need for atonement—reconciliation with the Divine and one another. The Day of Atonement speaks to the heart of our faith: the relentless pursuit of peace, justice, and the healing of relationships fractured by human failure. It underscores the necessity of humility, service, and compassion, essential virtues in our walk with God and our neighbors.

At its core, Leviticus 23:26-32 calls for a pause, a sacred halt in the ordinary pursuits of life, inviting us to reflect on our spiritual state and relationships. This pause is not a passive act but a dynamic engagement with the Divine, a moment to confront our shortcomings and seek renewal through God's grace. It is a time for deep self-examination to assess how we embody love, justice, and reconciliation daily.

In reflecting on this passage, we are drawn into the broader narrative of Scripture, which culminates in the person of Jesus Christ. Jesus embodies the ultimate atonement, bridging the chasm between humanity and the Divine through his love, sacrifice, and resurrection. His life and teachings provide the model for how we respond to Leviticus 23:26–32 themes. Through Jesus's example, we learn that to follow him is to walk in love, serve with humility, pursue justice, and extend forgiveness even to our enemies.

This passage is not a relic of a bygone era but an exciting call to live out our faith in the world today. It challenges us to consider how we, fueled by Jesus's love and empowered by the Spirit, can be agents of reconciliation and peace in our communities. How do we embody God's compassion and forgiveness in a world marked by division and strife?

Big Idea: Embrace humility and seek divine reconciliation to live out justice, peace, and love in daily life.

Reflection: How does our life reflect the call to reconciliation and service highlighted in Leviticus 23:26–32? How can we more fully embrace the model of Jesus to be peacemakers in our world?

Prayer: Divine Presence, please guide us to deeper reflection and renewal on this faith journey. Help us embrace the lessons of Leviticus 23:26–32: to live in humility, seek justice, and love with a compassion that reflects your heart. Empower us by your Spirit to be agents of reconciliation, following the path of Jesus, our example and guide. Amen.

Day 42

Journey of Joy

Reading: Leviticus 23:33-44

This passage is about the Feast of Booths. This festival, rich in symbolism and celebration, calls the community to recall their journey through the wilderness, living in temporary shelters, and rejoice in God's provision and faithfulness. It's a profound narrative that brings together memory, gratitude, and hope, offering us a multifaceted lens through which to view our spiritual quest today.

This ancient celebration speaks profoundly to our spiritual lives, reminding us of the impermanence of our earthly existence and the enduring faithfulness of the Divine. It calls us to a posture of humility and gratitude, recognizing that all we have is a gift. The Feast of Booths encourages us to remember our journeys and the moments of wilderness and to find joy in the provision and presence that has guided us. It's a reminder that, in our transient world, our ultimate home and hope lie beyond the temporal.

Leviticus 23:33-44 reflects on the past and guides us in how to live today. It encourages us to embody the values of peace, justice, reconciliation, and love. In remembering our dependence on divine provision, we are called to a life of service and compassion, extending hospitality and care to those around us, especially the marginalized and vulnerable. Celebrating the Feast of Booths in a communal setting underscores the importance of community and fellowship, reminding us that our faith journey is not solitary but shared with others, encouraging mutual support and love.

In the light of the New Testament, Jesus embodies the true meaning of the Feast of Booths. He is our ultimate shelter and sustenance, guiding us through our wilderness with his love, presence, spirit, and grace. Jesus invites us into a life of rejoicing in God's faithfulness, serving others with humility and love, and looking forward with hope to our eternal home. Through Jesus, we learn to live out the lessons of Leviticus 23:33-44, embodying the values of the kingdom of God in our everyday lives.

Big Idea: Live with gratitude and joy, serving others as we voyage towards our eternal home with God.

Reflection: How does remembering God's faithfulness in our past encourage us in our present journey? How can we embody the spirit of the Feast of Booths through service, hospitality, and community?

Prayer: Gracious God, remind us of your constant presence and provision throughout our pilgrimage. Help us to live in a spirit of gratitude, service, and joy, reflecting your love and grace to those around us. May we embody the lessons of the Feast of Booths, finding our ultimate hope and home in you. Amen.

Day 43

Eternal Light

Reading: Leviticus 24:1-9

Leviticus 24:1-9 introduces us to the commandment for the continual lighting of the lampstand and the setting of the bread of the Presence in the tabernacle. This passage, while deeply rooted in the liturgical practices of ancient Israel, transcends its historical context to speak into our spiritual lives today. It symbolizes the constant presence of God among God's people and the sustenance God provides, both physically and spiritually.

This command to keep the lamp burning continuously reminds us of the need for a persistent awareness of God's presence in our lives. Just as the lampstand was to be tended continually, so should our attention to our relationship with the Divine be constant and intentional. The bread of the Presence, set out weekly, speaks to the regularity with which we must come to God for our spiritual sustenance, recognizing that just as our bodies require food, our souls need nourishment from a close relationship with our Creator.

These rituals underscore themes of peace, justice, reconciliation, love, humility, service, faith, compassion, forgiveness, and the importance of community. In a world often marked by division and strife, continually turning towards God's light and seeking sustenance from God's presence compels us to live out these values. It calls us to be peacemakers, and to act justly, love mercy, and walk humbly with God, extending compassion and forgiveness to others. This passage invites us to reflect on how we can be a light in the darkness, embodying the love and grace that we receive from God in our interactions with others.

In the New Testament, Jesus declares himself to be the light of the world and the bread of life, fulfilling and transcending the symbols of the lampstand and the bread of the Presence. His life, death, and resurrection provide the ultimate example of how to live out the values highlighted in Leviticus 24:1–9. Through Jesus's love, presence, spirit, and grace, we are empowered to be his disciples, embodying his light, and sharing the sustenance we receive from him with the world.

Big Idea: Continually seek God's presence and share God's light and sustenance with the world.

Reflection: How can we better reflect God's light daily? What steps can we take to ensure we regularly come to God for spiritual sustenance?

Prayer: Loving God, help us remember your constant presence in our lives and to seek you daily for our spiritual nourishment. May your light within us shine brightly in a world needing your love and grace. Empower us to live out the values of peace, justice, and compassion, following the example of Jesus, our bread of life and light of the world. Amen.

Day 44

Sacred Words, Just Actions

Reading: Leviticus 24:10-23

Leviticus 24:10–23 presents a challenging and complex narrative about blasphemy, community responsibility, and the principles of justice. This passage recounts the story of a man who blasphemed the Name and the ensuing commandment for his punishment, alongside laws emphasizing equal justice under the law. At first glance, this text might seem distant from our contemporary context, yet it holds profound spiritual implications and ethical challenges for us today.

The biblical narrative underscores the sanctity of the divine name, reflecting the profound reverence and respect due to the Creator. This passage challenges Christians to live in a way that honors the sacredness of God's name through our words and actions, to pursue justice that reflects God's mercy, and to foster a community where peace and reconciliation prevail. Leviticus 24 also establishes a principle of justice that was revolutionary for its time: the idea of equal retribution, encapsulated in the phrase, "eye for an eye." This was not a call to vengeance but a boundary against excessive punishment, ensuring the penalty would not exceed the crime. This concept of justice, rooted in equality and fairness, challenges us to consider how we enact justice in our communities and lives.

Spiritually, this passage prompts us to reflect on the nature of our speech and the respect we hold for the sacred. It invites us to consider the power of our words and their impact on our community and relationship with the Divine. Emphasizing equitable justice speaks to our spiritual call to pursue fair and compassionate justice, recognizing every person's inherent value.

In light of the New Testament, Jesus's teachings and actions radically reinterpret these principles. Jesus calls us to love our enemies, to offer forgiveness, and to seek reconciliation. His life exemplifies a justice rooted in love and mercy rather than mere retribution. Through his example, we are invited to embody a community that speaks with reverence, acts with integrity, and administers justice with compassion.

Big Idea: Honor the sacred with our words and enact justice with mercy, guided by Jesus's example.

Reflection: How do we use our words to honor or dishonor the Divine? How does our understanding of justice align with the principles of mercy and love demonstrated by Jesus?

Prayer: Just and merciful God, please guide us to use our words wisely and with reverence for your holy name. Help us to understand and practice justice in a way that reflects your love and mercy. Empower us to be agents of reconciliation in our communities, following the example of Jesus, who taught us to love unconditionally. Amen.

Day 45

Rhythms of Rest

Reading: Leviticus 25:1–7

Leviticus 25:1–7 introduces the Sabbath year, a divine command for the land to rest every seventh year. While deeply agricultural in its immediate context, this passage sows seeds of profound spiritual truth for our lives today. It calls for a rhythm of work and rest, not only for the benefit of the land but as a reminder of our reliance on God's provision and the importance of sustainable living.

This commandment underscores a fundamental principle: the earth is the Lord's. As stewards of God's creation we are challenged to consider our relationship with the environment and the resources entrusted to us. The Sabbath year serves as a reminder that true productivity and sustainability are found not in relentless toil but in balanced rhythms of work and rest, echoing the creation narrative where God rested on the seventh day.

For our spiritual lives, Leviticus 25:1–7 invites us into a deeper understanding of rest in God. It encourages us to trust in God's provision, to release our grip on control and productivity, and to find our worth not in what we do but in whom we belong to. This passage calls us to a lifestyle of humility and dependence on God, recognizing that God's grace sustains our efforts.

This ancient practice informs in profound ways how Christians should live. It speaks to the importance of creating spaces of rest and renewal in our lives and communities, fostering environments where people and the earth can flourish. It challenges us to live out justice, showing care for the creation and consideration for future generations. The principles of the Sabbath year propel us towards actions of peace, reconciliation, and love as we recognize our shared responsibility for stewardship and our common dependence on God's provision.

In the light of the New Testament, Jesus embodies the proper rest promised by God. He invites us to a Sabbath rest in him, offering relief from our burdens and the weight of striving. Jesus teaches us that our ultimate rest and sustenance come from God alone. His presence, love, spirit, and grace enable us to live out the themes of Leviticus 25:1–7, guiding us in practices of rest, stewardship, and sustainable living that honor God and serve our neighbors.

Big Idea: Embrace rest and stewardship as faith in God's provision and care for creation.

Reflection: How can we incorporate rhythms of rest and trust in God's provision into our lives? How does our stewardship of the earth reflect our relationship with the Creator?

Prayer: God who provides and cares, please teach us to find rest in you and to trust in your provision. Guide us in living responsibly and sustainably, caring for your creation and one another as stewards of the gifts you have given us. Help us live in the rhythms of grace Jesus exemplified, finding our worth and sustenance in your love. Amen.

Day 46

Grace in Jubilee

Reading: Leviticus 25:8-34

Leviticus 25:8-34 introduces the Jubilee Year, a divine command for the Israelites to proclaim liberty throughout the land every fiftieth year. This period was marked by the return of all property to its original owners and the release of all indentured servants. The Jubilee embodies profound principles of freedom, restoration, and economic justice, offering a radical vision of community and kinship under God.

The Jubilee Year is a powerful metaphor for God's redemption and grace, reflecting a divine concern for equity and compassion. It reminds us that our time, resources, and relationships are under God's sovereign care. This passage challenges us to consider how we, as stewards of God's creation, participate in systems of justice and mercy. It calls us to reflect on our responsibility towards the marginalized and oppressed, urging us to take actionable steps towards creating communities that mirror God's kingdom of peace, justice, and reconciliation.

In our spiritual lives, Leviticus 25:8-34 invites us to embrace the principles of the Jubilee as a way of life. It encourages us to periodically assess our lives and societies, to identify where bondage and inequality persist, and to take steps towards liberation and restoration. This passage calls us into a deeper relationship with God, where we recognize our dependence on God's provision and grace and are motivated to live out God's commandments in ways that promote dignity, respect, and love for all.

The Jubilee Year's themes resonate with the teachings and ministry of Jesus, who proclaimed good news to the poor and freedom for the oppressed. Jesus embodies the ultimate Jubilee, offering spiritual liberation and restoration to all who come to him. Through his life, death, and resurrection, Jesus demonstrates the extent of God's love and the transformative power of grace. As followers of Christ, we are invited to participate in this ongoing work of Jubilee, becoming agents of freedom and reconciliation in a broken world.

Big Idea: Cultivate a lifestyle of generosity and restoration, reflecting God's grace through Jubilee practices.

Reflection: How can we embody the spirit of the Jubilee in our contexts? What steps can we take to promote justice, freedom, and restoration in our communities and beyond?

Prayer: Lord God, inspire us to live in the spirit of the Jubilee, seeking justice, practicing mercy, and walking humbly with you. Grant us the wisdom and courage to create communities that reflect your love and grace. Help us to follow the example of Jesus, who calls us to proclaim liberty and restoration in your name. Amen.

Day 47

Compassion in Action

Reading: Leviticus 25:35-54

Leviticus 25:35-54 reflects God's vision for community, emphasizing support, redemption, and freedom. This portion of Scripture outlines God's instructions for the Israelites on how to treat fellow Israelites who have fallen into poverty or have had to sell themselves into servitude. It commands the people of God to lend to the needy without interest, to treat bondsmen as hired workers rather than enslaved people, and to outline the right of redemption for both people and property. This passage is not merely a set of ancient laws but a divine blueprint for compassion, justice, and liberation within the community.

At its core, Leviticus 25:35-54 teaches us about the nature of God's kingdom, where care for the vulnerable and practicing justice is paramount. It challenges us to see beyond our personal needs and comforts, urging us to embody a community that reflects God's heart for the oppressed and the marginalized. This passage calls us to radical hospitality and generosity, reminding us that our resources are not our own but are given by God to steward for the welfare of the entire community.

The principles found in these verses are as relevant today as they were in ancient Israel. They compel us to ask how we support those in need and work towards liberating those oppressed by debt, poverty, and systemic injustice. It invites us to consider our role in fostering a community where everyone has the opportunity for redemption and a fresh start. This is the essence of living out the gospel—a gospel that proclaims release to the captives and recovery of sight to the blind, a gospel that is lived out not just in words but in actions of love, service, and justice.

Jesus embodies and fulfills these principles of care, redemption, and liberation. He announced the coming of God's kingdom, where the last are first, and the first, last, and where the hungry are fed, the naked clothed, and strangers welcomed. Through his life, death, and resurrection, Jesus demonstrates the ultimate act of redemption, offering us freedom from the bondage of sin and inviting us into a life of discipleship that mirrors his compassion and justice.

Big Idea: Live generously, embodying God's compassion and justice to uplift and liberate the vulnerable.

Reflection: How are we contributing to a community that reflects God's kingdom? How does our treatment of the vulnerable and marginalized align with Jesus's example?

Prayer: Generous, compassionate, and just God, please guide us to live by your teachings, showing love, compassion, and justice to all. Please help us to see those in need through your eyes and to respond with generosity and kindness. Empower us by your Spirit to be agents of redemption and freedom, following the example of Jesus, in whose name we pray. Amen.

Day 48

Covenant Blessings

Reading: Leviticus 26:1-13

Leviticus 26:1-13 unfolds with a divine promise of blessings for obedience, a covenantal reminder that faithfulness to God's commands brings harmony between the Creator and creation. This passage outlines a series of blessings that will follow the Israelites should they remain faithful to God's statutes, including rain in due season, bountiful harvests, peace in the land, victory over enemies, and most importantly, God's indwelling presence among them. These promises are not merely material but signify a deeper spiritual reality: living by God's will brings about a life that flourishes in every dimension.

For our spiritual lives today, this passage echoes the timeless truth that our relationship with God is foundational to all aspects of life. It reminds us that obedience to God's will is not about legalistic adherence to rules but about aligning our lives with the divine design for creation, which leads to true flourishing. This alignment brings peace, provision, and presence—core aspects of the kingdom of God that Jesus preached and lived.

Living out the teachings of Leviticus 26:1-13 today means embodying the principles of peace, justice, reconciliation, love, humility, service, faith, compassion, and forgiveness in our daily interactions. It challenges us to consider how our lives reflect God's kingdom values, urging us to be agents of peace in a world rife with conflict, to seek justice for the oppressed, to love and serve our neighbors, and to extend forgiveness as we have been forgiven. This passage calls us to a holistic faith that not only believes in God's promises but actively works towards realizing the vision of God's kingdom on earth.

In the New Testament, Jesus embodies the fulfillment of these covenantal blessings, offering peace, provision, and eternal life through his death and resurrection. Jesus Christ invites us into a relationship with him, where his love, presence, spirit, and grace enable us to live out the principles outlined in Leviticus. Jesus, through his Spirit, empowers us to be disciples who enjoy God's blessings and extend them to others.

Big Idea: Live faithfully to manifest God's peace, provision, and presence in and through our lives.

Reflection: How does our faithfulness to God's commands reflect our pursuit of peace, justice, and love in our communities? In what ways are we experiencing God's presence in our lives as a result of living in obedience to God's will?

Prayer: Gracious and loving God, please help us obey your commands so that we might experience the fullness of your blessings. Empower us by your Spirit to be bearers of peace, justice, and love, reflecting the life of Jesus in our words and actions. May we be mindful of your presence, guiding us to live harmoniously with your will. Amen.

Day 49

Pathways of Repentance

Reading: Leviticus 26:14-46

Leviticus 26:14-46 presents a sobering counterpart to the blessings outlined in the preceding verses, detailing the consequences of disobedience to God's commands. This passage, while stark, is not merely about punishment but is deeply rooted in the covenantal relationship between God and God's people. It underscores the seriousness with which God views disobedience, not because of a desire to inflict harm but because of a commitment to holiness, justice, and the community's well-being. The curses described are a call back to faithfulness, a reminder that actions have consequences, and an invitation to repentance and restoration.

For our spiritual lives, this passage serves as a poignant reminder of the importance of obedience, the reality of God's justice, and the ever-present opportunity for repentance. It challenges us to examine our lives, consider where we might be straying from God's path, and recognize how our actions impact our relationship with God and those around us. This portion of Scripture invites us to a deeper understanding of God's holiness and desire for people to live in a way that reflects God's character.

In response to Leviticus 26:14-46, Christians are called to live with an awareness of the communal implications of our actions.

This passage informs our pursuit of peace, justice, reconciliation, love, humility, service, faith, compassion, and forgiveness. It reminds us that these virtues are not optional extras but central to our covenantal relationship with God. Living in light of these themes means actively working against injustice, seeking reconciliation in our relationships, practicing humility and service, and extending forgiveness. It is about embodying the love of Christ in a broken world, recognizing that we are empowered to do so not by our strength but through the grace and presence of Jesus.

Jesus stands at the heart of our response to the challenges of Leviticus 26:14–46. In Christ, we find the perfect example of obedience to God's will, the ultimate expression of love, and how we are reconciled to God. Jesus's life, death, and resurrection assure us of God's forgiveness and provide the foundation for our efforts to live by God's commands. Through Christ, we are not only recipients of grace but also agents of reconciliation and peace.

Big Idea: Embrace repentance and live out God's justice and love, empowered by the grace of Jesus.

Reflection: Where might we seek repentance and restoration? How can we more fully embody the virtues of peace, justice, and love in our communities?

Prayer: Gracious Creator God, grant us the courage to face our shortcomings and the grace to turn back to you. Help us to cultivate lives that reflect your holiness and love, guided by the example of Jesus and empowered by your Spirit. May we be instruments of your peace and reconciliation in the world. Amen.

Day 50

Devoted Integrity

Reading: Leviticus 27

Leviticus 27, the concluding chapter of this profound book, addresses vows and dedications made to God. It outlines how individuals can dedicate people, animals, or property to the Lord and the value or redemption of these vows. This passage emphasizes the seriousness with which vows to God should be treated, reflecting the importance of commitment and the integrity of one's word. It teaches us about the value God places on the offerings of God's people—not just in material terms but as expressions of devotion and worship.

For our spiritual lives, Leviticus 27 reminds us of the significance of our commitments to God. It challenges us to consider the vows we make, whether in moments of prayer, during times of worship, or in the quiet of our hearts. This passage invites us to reflect on how we honor these commitments daily, reminding us that our offerings to God are about more than fulfilling obligations; they are expressions of our love and devotion to the One who has given us everything.

This chapter also speaks to how Christians should live, emphasizing principles such as integrity, generosity, and the sanctity of our commitments to God and one another. It calls us to live with integrity and sincerity. In a broader sense, Leviticus 27 encourages us to consider how we dedicate our lives to God's service—how we use our time, talents, and resources to honor God and advance God's kingdom. It challenges us to live with a spirit of generosity, recognizing that everything we have is a gift from God and will be used for God's glory and the good of others.

In the New Testament, Jesus amplifies the themes of Leviticus 27, teaching about the cost of discipleship and the importance of counting the cost before committing (Luke 14:28–33). He also warns against making vows lightly (Matthew 5:33–37). Through his life and ministry, Jesus exemplifies the ultimate dedication to God's will, showing us how to live our lives as a sacrifice, holy and pleasing to God (Romans 12:1).

Big Idea: Honor God with sincere commitments, pursuing lives of integrity and generosity as expressions of devotion.

Reflection: What vows or commitments have we made to God, and how are we honoring them? How does our dedication to God reflect how we live and use our resources?

Prayer: Holy and loving God, help us to live with integrity and generosity, honoring our commitments to you and others. May our offerings, whether of time, talent, or treasure, reflect our love and devotion to you. Guide us by your Spirit to live in a manner worthy of the calling we have received, following the example of Jesus, in whose name we pray. Amen.

Appendix 1

Daily Devotions with Jesus Devotional Books and Podcast

DAILY DEVOTIONS WITH JESUS aims to help you understand and respond to the Bible, grow spiritually, and learn how to impact the world as a follower of Jesus Christ. After all, these devotions aren't just about learning about the Bible. They are also about growing ever more deeply in love with Jesus and following him with every fiber of your being and in every area of your life.

The Daily Devotions with Jesus devotional books and podcast offer a rich, engaging, and spiritually nourishing experience.

Podcast Links:

https://linktr.ee/dailydevotions
https://grahamjosephhill.com/devotions
https://www.youtube.com/@GrahamJosephHill_Author

Features:

The Daily Devotions with Jesus podcast offers a wide range of engaging and beneficial features:

1. **Daily Episodes:** Each episode, lasting around ten minutes, focuses on a specific Bible chapter or set of verses. Each

episode offers a devotion designed to enrich your spiritual life.

2. **Covering the While Bible:** The episodes move through the Bible, from Genesis to Revelation.

3. **Guided Prayers:** Each episode offers a prayer tailored to the day's Bible reading, encouraging spiritual growth and personal reflection.

4. **Flexible Pace:** The podcast offers relaxed and flexible pacing, allowing you to go deeper into each chapter or set of verses.

5. **Devotional Books:** You can also get the devotional books accompanying this podcast, which are excellent for personal and group study (see https://grahamjosephhill.com/books).

6. **Bible Reading Plan:** You can follow the Bible Reading Plan at https://grahamjosephhill.com/biblereadingplan.

7. **Listening Options:** To listen on a range of podcasting platforms see https://linktr.ee/dailydevotions.

Appendix 2

Bible Reading Plan

GrahamJosephHill.com/BibleReadingPlan

This Bible Reading Plan shows you how to read the entire Bible, exploring each chapter's themes in depth.

Each day you will read a chapter or set of verses and the devotional book dedicated to the book of the Bible you're reading and you can tune into the accompanying Daily Devotions with Jesus podcast episode.

Tips for Staying on Track:

1. **Keep the Goal in Mind:** The goal is to grow ever more deeply in love with Jesus and follow him with every fiber of your being and in every area of your life.
2. **Set a Specific Time:** Dedicate a specific time of the day to read and listen to the podcast episode.
3. **Reflect and Pray:** Take time to reflect on the chapter or set of verses and pray.
4. **Keep a Journal:** Note down your thoughts or insights from each day's reading.

5. **Seek Understanding:** If a chapter or set of verses are difficult to understand, consider consulting the Daily Devotions with Jesus devotional book dedicated to the book of the Bible you're reading.
6. **Stay Committed:** It's a long journey but staying committed will be rewarding.
7. **Explore the Bible with Others:** Discussing the Bible and devotions in groups can help keep you on track and make your experience more rewarding.
8. **Go Gentle on Yourself:** If you miss a day, go gentle on yourself. You can pick up reading tomorrow. Grace is at the heart of our relationship with Jesus.

The Bible Reading Plan

See the Bible Reading Plan at GrahamJosephHill/BibleReadingPlan. This will be updated as each book of the Bible is completed for the devotional books and podcast.

Appendix 3

Other Books and Resources by Graham Joseph Hill

Author and Ministry Websites

Linktr.ee/dailydevotions
GrahamJosephHill.com
youtube.com/@GrahamJosephHill_Author

Books

Healing Our Broken Humanity: Practices for Revitalizing the Church and Renewing the World. Downers Grove, IL: InterVarsity, 2018 (with Grace Ji-Sun Kim).

Hide This in Your Heart: Memorizing Scripture for Kingdom Impact. Colorado Springs, CO: NavPress, 2020 (with Michael Frost).

Holding Up Half the Sky: A Biblical Case for Women Leading and Teaching in the Church. Eugene, OR: Cascade, 2020.

Salt, Light, and a City, Second Edition: Conformation—Ecclesiology for the Global Missional Community: Volume 2, Majority World Voices. Eugene, OR: Cascade, 2020.

Salt, Light, and a City, Second Edition: Ecclesiology for the Global Missional Community: Volume 1, Western Voices. Eugene, OR: Cascade, 2017.

The Soul Online: Bereavement, Social Media, and Competent Care. Eugene, OR: Wipf and Stock, 2022 (with Desiree Geldenhuys).

Sunburnt Country, Sweeping Pains: The Experiences of Asian Australian Women in Ministry and Mission. Eugene, OR: Wipf and Stock, 2022.

World Christianity: An Introduction. Eugene, OR: Cascade, 2024.

www.ingramcontent.com/pod-product-compliance
Lightning Source LLC
Chambersburg PA
CBHW060031180426
43196CB00044B/2369